The Panama Canal

The Panama
Canal

Other titles in the *History's Great Structures* series include:

History's Great
STRUCTURES

The Panama Canal

Stephen Currie

ReferencePoint
Press®

San Diego, CA

© 2015 ReferencePoint Press, Inc.
Printed in the United States

For more information, contact:
ReferencePoint Press, Inc.
PO Box 27779
San Diego, CA 92198
www.ReferencePointPress.com

LIBRARY OF CONGRESS CATALOGING-IN-PUBLICATION DATA

Currie, Stephen, 1960-
The Panama Canal / by Stephen Currie.
pages cm. -- (History's great structures series)
Includes bibliographical references and index.
ISBN 978-1-60152-710-3 (hardback) -- ISBN 1-60152-710-1 (hardback)
1. Panama Canal (Panama)--History--Juvenile literature. I. Title.
F1569.C2C87   2014
386'.44--dc23
                                                                    2014020644

CONTENTS

IMPORTANT EVENTS IN THE HISTORY OF THE PANAMA CANAL

1881
A French company begins work on the Panama Canal.

1914
The Panama Canal is completed.

1906
Yellow fever is virtually wiped out in Panama.

1859
Work begins on the Suez Canal.

1903
The Panamanian revolution begins and ends.

1860　　　　1880　　　　1900

1869
The Suez Canal is completed.

1912
Riots break out at Cocoa Grove.

1888
Work on the Panama Canal is abandoned.

1898
The USS *Oregon* travels around Cape Horn.

1904
The United States begins work on the Panama Canal.

2014
The Panama Canal celebrates its hundredth year of operation.

1955
A new treaty is signed by the United States and Panama.

1978
Two new treaties are signed by Panamanian and US leaders.

2007
The Panama Canal Expansion project begins.

1960   1980   2000

1964
Riots break out in the Canal Zone over the flying of flags.

1999
The Panama Canal is officially transferred to Panama.

2013
Nicaragua announces plans to build a canal across its territory.

1979
The Canal Zone is abolished.

The Canal

Around the second century BCE, several Greek writers compiled a list of impressive structures in the Mediterranean Sea region. Seven structures in all appeared on the list, including the Great Pyramid of Giza in Egypt, the Hanging Gardens of Babylon, and an enormous statue of the Greek god Zeus at Olympia in Greece. The structures were collectively called the Seven Wonders of the World. In modern times, following this ancient tradition, it has become common for people to refer to various newer structures as the "Eighth Wonder of the World." Over the years this label has been applied to architectural marvels such as the Empire State Building in New York City; the Houston Astrodome; the opera house in Sydney, Australia; and the Three Gorges Dam that spans the Yangtze River in China.

The Joining of Oceans

The title of "Eighth Wonder of the World" has also been widely—and justifiably—used to describe another structure: the Panama Canal. Joining the Atlantic and Pacific Oceans through the small Central American country of Panama, the Panama Canal runs about 48 miles (77 km) through hilly, rocky rain forest in a hot and humid region that has been described as among the least hospitable on earth. The waterway was designed by American engineers and built by laborers from many different countries. Construction on the canal was plagued by any number of problems, from rockslides to accidents involving dynamite and from unceasing rainfall to mosquitoes that carried deadly disease. The building process required ten years, tens of thousands of workers, and several hundred million dollars; the goal was to complete a project unlike any that had ever been accomplished.

Yet the project was not only completed, it was finished on time and under budget. In August 1914, as scheduled, the Panama Canal formally opened, with the American steamship *Ancon* making the first official trip through the waterway. The Atlantic and Pacific Oceans had been linked. To observers everything about the canal seemed impressive. The canal's overall design, which included several sets of locks intended to raise and lower ships as they made their way from one end of the canal to the other, struck many as brilliant. So did the recycling of dirt and gravel excavated from the path of the canal to create embankments and make concrete. The size of the locks, the length of the canal, the countless hours of labor that had been needed to create the waterway—all of these seemed to be on a different scale from what most people were used to in the early 1900s, and all helped earn the canal the designation of one of the world's great wonders.

The canal was indeed impressive, well worth the accolades it has received both then and now. However, the canal has always been more than just a remarkable structure. On the contrary, the Panama Canal has had great cultural and political significance as well. Built in a time when the United States was becoming a force in world affairs, the canal seemed to many Americans to be a clear representation of American ingenuity, American know-how, and a distinctively American spirit. The fact that the United States had successfully completed this difficult project struck many Americans as an important indicator of the nation's rising power around the globe.

Controversies

At the same time, though, the completion of the canal brought decidedly mixed emotions to the people of another country: Panama,

The Canal Zone

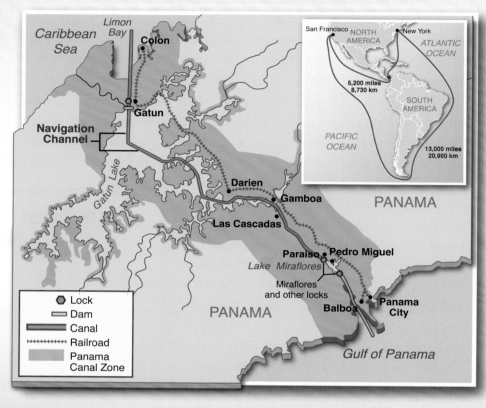

The Panama Canal created a shortcut from the Atlantic Ocean to the Pacific.

Caribbean Sea

Limon Bay

Colon

Gatun

Navigation Channel

Gatun Lake

Darien

Gamboa

Las Cascadas

Paraiso

Pedro Miguel

Lake Miraflores

Miraflores and other locks

Balboa

Panama City

PANAMA

Gulf of Panama

Legend:
- Lock
- Dam
- Canal
- Railroad
- Panama Canal Zone

San Francisco

NORTH AMERICA

New York

ATLANTIC OCEAN

5,200 miles
8,730 km

SOUTH AMERICA

PACIFIC OCEAN

13,000 miles
20,900 km

PANAMA

the nation through which the waterway ran. Though the coming of the Americans had been in many ways quite beneficial to the Panamanians—indeed, it had helped give them a country of their own—many Panamanians were angered by the Americans' overall attitude toward them. The Americans had taken some of their territory and seemed uninterested in listening to the natives' complaints. These concerns, unaddressed for the most part by the US government, would fester for years and result in riots aimed at the American presence in Panama. In the end, after many years and much negotiation, the entire operation would be put in Panamanian hands.

Through the years, the canal has been a clear success. Day after day it moves ships from one ocean to the other, a process that can take as little as eight to ten hours. Accidents are rare, and closures are almost unknown. In 2010 the canal closed briefly when unusually heavy rainfall caused floods that made the channel unsafe for shipping; it was the first time the canal had been shut down, even briefly, in twenty-one years. The Panama Canal has remained open despite natural disasters, diplomatic crises, and two world wars. With ships from all over the world moving through the locks to ports around the globe, the canal is an enduring symbol of the connections between nations and—especially now that the canal is in Panamanian hands—the ability of human beings to work together in friendship and peace.

With the exception of the Great Pyramid of Giza in Egypt, all of the original Seven Wonders of the World are gone or lie

in ruins. While the Panama Canal has some issues—age, size, and the threat of competition from another Central American canal among them—it does not seem likely to meet the same fate any time soon. Even though the economic and strategic importance of the canal has diminished since its completion in 1914, the waterway still serves as a valuable shortcut for commercial freighters and other vessels. And as the canal celebrates its hundredth anniversary, it is being significantly refurbished to open it to ever-larger ships that make up an increasing percentage of the world's fleet. The canal ranks among the most remarkable—and useful—pieces of architecture anywhere in the world. From its planning and design to its construction and the political controversies that surrounded it in the late twentieth century, it has undoubtedly deserved the attention it has been given over the years.

CHAPTER ONE

A Plan

The continents of North and South America stretch for more than 8,000 miles (12,875 km) from top to bottom, forming a barrier for ships attempting to cross between the Atlantic and Pacific Oceans. Sailors from the 1500s on were forced to follow an extremely circuitous route that brought them around Cape Horn at the southern tip of South America. That added several days to the journey of even the fastest ship trying to move from the northern part of one ocean to the northern part of the other. That path is also dangerous. The winds and currents off Cape Horn are ferocious, and many ships over the years have been smashed to bits against the cape's rocky shores.

Since the Cape Horn route was risky and inefficient, seafarers and explorers tried to find an alternative. Between the 1600s and the 1800s, many adventurers traveled in the Arctic regions along the top of North America, looking for an ice-free Northwest Passage that would enable ships to move freely between the two oceans. By the late nineteenth century, though, it was becoming increasingly clear that the Northwest Passage either did not exist or was so full of ice that even in the summer it would not be a reliable route for shipping. More and more, explorers were agreeing with Thomas James, an explorer of the 1600s, who had doubted that such a passage existed. "In all probability," James had written, "there is no Northwest Passage to the south sea [the Pacific]."[1]

With the southerly route unappealing and the northerly route unavailable, the only remaining possibility was to go directly through the landmass. Though both North and South America extend a long way from west to east—about 4,000 miles (6,437 km) in the case of North America—the land narrows considerably where the two continents come together in Central America. Geographers describe a narrow landmass between two oceans or seas as an isthmus, and the southernmost portion of Central America certainly fits that description. In particular, the modern country of Panama qualifies as an isthmus. Though Panama stretches more than 700 miles (1,127 km) along its coastlines, it is rarely much more than 40 miles (64 km) wide. The land was mountainous and swampy; still, some observers believed it possible to dig a canal that would slice Panama in two and provide a quick and easy path between the oceans.

Early History

The idea of a canal was not new. As early as the 1500s the king of Spain had suggested that a canal might be constructed across the Panamanian isthmus. Though the canal would have helped Spain tighten its colonial hold on South America, the technology of the day was not equal to the challenge of constructing one. "All the gold in the world would not suffice for its execution,"[2] the Spanish governor of Panama warned the king, and the idea went nowhere. In the late 1700s an Italian sea captain named Alessandro Malaspina not only argued that a canal would be a good idea, but he described how the waterway might be excavated. The time, however, was still not ripe, and Malaspina's proposal was more or less forgotten.

WORDS IN CONTEXT
isthmus
A narrow piece of land between two bodies of water.

As technology and trade increased, though, the notion of a canal across the Panamanian isthmus seemed increasingly feasible—and necessary. The Suez Canal, which ran between Africa and Asia and connected the Mediterranean Sea to the Red Sea, was completed in 1869; this canal permitted ships to move directly from Europe to Asia without having to sail all the way around Africa. The Suez Canal was

The rocky coast of Cape Horn in South America was treacherous for ships that sailed around it. The Panama Canal would eliminate the need for the voyage around Cape Horn.

an impressive engineering feat, stretching as it did more than 100 miles (161 km) across the desert. Though it was not an immediate financial success—despite the use of what amounted to slave labor, it cost about twice what original estimates had projected—it had an immediate impact on trade, with ships cutting days off their journeys by using the canal instead of the traditional southern route. To many people the example of the Suez Canal proved that a canal across Panama was a realistic goal.

One of those people was a French diplomat named Ferdinand de Lesseps. De Lesseps had helped to spearhead the building of the Suez Canal, and he firmly believed that a similar canal could be constructed across the much shorter isthmus of Panama. Through the 1870s he attempted to drum up support for a Panamanian canal among engineers, investors, and government officials, eventually forming a company to support him in this endeavor. In 1881 construction began.

The project did not go well, however. The hot, wet climate proved difficult for workers to manage, the engineering difficulties of digging a canal through the mountains were overwhelming, and tropical diseases such as malaria and yellow fever killed thousands of laborers. The project was underfunded, moreover, and that problem was compounded by financial mismanagement and corruption. In December 1888 construction was stopped on the canal altogether.

The Voyage of the *Oregon*

Over the next ten years, there was little interest in attempting to continue building a canal across the isthmus. Then in 1898 war broke out between Spain and the United States. As part of the war effort, America decided to send a battleship called the USS *Oregon* to the Caribbean, where US forces were trying to wrest control of Cuba from Spain. Unfortunately, the *Oregon* was stationed at Bremerton, Washington, which was on the northern Pacific coast. It took the ship more than two months to reach the Caribbean by way of Cape Horn. As it turned out, though, the ship arrived in time to take part in an important naval battle, and the *Oregon* helped win the war for the United States.

Still, to many American leaders the experience was sobering. The United States was rapidly becoming a world power, with influence in

COATS OF ARMS AND POSTAGE STAMPS

In the early 1900s, when the US government decided to build a Central American canal, locating it in Panama rather than Nicaragua was not an automatic decision. In the end Panama was chosen because the route was shorter, because the French were interested in selling their survey work and equipment—and because of a volcano.

One of the strongest supporters of a Panamanian route was Frenchman Philippe Bunau-Varilla. Bunau-Varilla repeatedly lobbied Congress to choose this route. He had a dual strategy: emphasizing Panama's benefits and pointing out Nicaragua's weaknesses. Among the latter, as Bunau-Varilla saw it, was Nicaragua's location in a region with active volcanoes. He tried to convince legislators that since an exploding volcano would block shipping, Panama was a far better choice. As he wrote in a pamphlet he distributed to influential leaders throughout the United States, "Look at the coat of arms of the Republic of Nicaragua; look at the Nicaraguan postage stamps. Young nations like to put on their coats of arms what best . . . characterizes their native soil. What have the Nicaraguans chosen to characterize their country on their coat of arms, on their postage stamps? Volcanoes!"

In June 1902 a Nicaraguan volcano named Momotombo erupted, making Bunau-Varilla's warning seem prescient. Historian David McCullough, among others, believes that the Panama route would have been chosen at that point regardless of the volcano—but the timely eruption certainly did not hurt.

Quoted in David McCullough, *The Path Between the Seas*. New York: Simon & Schuster, 1977, p. 285.

both the Atlantic and the Pacific. In this new world it might be necessary to transfer battleships from one ocean to the other at a moment's notice. To wait weeks or months for a ship to actually make its appearance seemed unacceptable. Had there been a canal across Panama, the *Oregon*'s journey would have been about 8,000 miles (12,875 km) shorter than it was, and it would have arrived considerably earlier than it did. For military reasons, American leaders decided it was essential to revisit the notion of a Central American canal. The question was whether the United States could succeed where the French had failed.

At first the United States considered building a canal not through Panama, but rather through Nicaragua, further north along the coast. The United States had already made one brief attempt to construct a Nicaraguan canal. Though the oceans were farther apart in Nicaragua than in Panama, the mountains were lower, and builders could connect the canal to a large lake located about halfway along the route. In 1902, though, de Lesseps's company offered to sell the United States all its assets in Panama, including heavy equipment, information from surveys of the region, and the areas that workers had managed to excavate. When the United States complained that the $109 million asking price was too high, the company lowered it to $40 million, and the deal was quickly completed.

Revolution

Several important issues remained, however. Chief among them was the need to negotiate a treaty with Colombia, the South American country that controlled Panama at the time. The proposed canal, after all, would cross Colombian territory, and the Colombian government, as it had with the French company two decades before, demanded compensation for allowing the Americans to build a canal. The US government thought that Colombia's price was too high, but Colombia refused to negotiate further. When the United States in turn declined to alter its own offer, the Colombian government rejected the treaty. Theodore Roosevelt, the US president at the time, was furious. Colombia, he thundered, could not be permitted to block "one of the future highways of civilization."[3] Indeed, he added, Colombian leadership amounted to nothing but "a government of irresponsible bandits."[4]

Getting around this problem, however, turned out to be easy. Many Panamanians were unhappy under Colombian rule. Panama was sparsely populated, relatively poor, and distant from the Colombian capital in Bogotá, and residents of the isthmus believed they were ignored by their government. In fact, there was a strong independence movement among Panamanians. The US government unofficially let the dissidents know that it would support an armed revolt should there be an insurrection against the Colombian government. The rebels also received considerable assistance from a French engineer named Philippe Bunau-Varilla, who had worked on the first attempt to build the canal and was eager to continue what he called "the great idea of Panama."[5] Bunau-Varilla not only talked up the rebels' cause in the United States, but he gave the rebels $100,000 of his own money as well.

In November 1903 the revolution began. Though the United States did not officially declare war on Colombia, there was no doubt about which side it was on, and the Americans wasted no time before flexing their muscles as the world's newest superpower. "By an interesting coincidence," author Jeremy Sherman Snapp writes wryly, "the cruiser USS *Nashville* just happened to be at Colón [a Panamanian city] during the uprising and was soon joined by the cruiser USS *Atlanta*, the new battleship USS *Maine*, the presidential yacht *Mayflower*, the USS *Prairie*, and the USS *Dixie*."[6] The Colombian government realized it had no chance of stopping the much more powerful American military and withdrew from the isthmus altogether. Three days after the revolution began it was over, and the United States became the first foreign country to recognize the new Panamanian republic.

Negotiating a Treaty

Roosevelt then assigned Secretary of State John Hay to negotiate a treaty with Panama. Hay's Panamanian counterpart was Bunau-Varilla, who though French was nevertheless appointed to represent Panamanian interests. Bunau-Varilla was so eager to get the canal built that he quickly agreed to almost every American demand. Afterward, many Panamanians blamed Bunau-Varilla for giving the United States too much and getting too little in return. In fairness to Bunau-Varilla, though, it is not clear that any Panamanian could have done a better job. The country, after all, existed only because the

French diplomat Ferdinand de Lesseps was involved in the building of the Suez Canal (pictured in this oil painting). He believed a similar canal could easily be built across the Isthmus of Panama.

United States had helped it break away from Colombia. If the United States turned its back on the Panamanians it was entirely possible that Colombia would try to reclaim the isthmus for itself. Panama therefore had very little leverage in negotiation.

Certainly the agreement was extremely favorable to the United States. The contract established a special Canal Zone within Panama, to be administered by the United States. This zone would extend from sea to sea roughly 5 miles (8 km) to each side of the canal. In essence, the Canal Zone was US territory and would be forever. The establishment of the Canal Zone had the effect of dividing Panama into two separate parts. The agreement also provided that the United States could bring military force to bear on Panama if it felt that riots or other conflicts might endanger the canal. Intervention, the agreement read, would be justified "in case the Republic of Panama should not be, in the judgment of the United States, able to maintain such order."[7]

Panama did receive some benefit from the deal. The United States agreed to pay the Panamanian government a fee of $10 million for the Canal Zone and for the right to build a canal—far less than the value of the land and the projected value of the waterway, but a siz-

A MODEL FOR PANAMA

Canals date back hundreds of years. The Grand Canal in China, which today runs more than 1,000 miles (1,609 km) from the Yangtze River to Beijing, was begun more than two thousand years ago. The Italian city of Venice is famous for its extensive network of canals, which for centuries have served as the city's streets. And the Erie Canal across New York State was constructed in the early 1800s as a shortcut for moving goods from the Great Lakes region to the port of New York City.

The canal that most influenced the decision to build the Panama Canal, however, was the Suez Canal, which runs from the Red Sea to the Mediterranean Sea through present-day Egypt. Designed by Ferdinand de Lesseps, who later tried to build a canal across the Panamanian isthmus, the canal was begun in 1859 and completed ten years later.

In most ways the Suez Canal was much easier to build than the Panama Canal was. Most notably, it was built across relatively flat terrain; thus, it required no locks, and workers essentially dug a ditch connecting the two seas. In another way, though, Suez was a more difficult operation. The machinery available to the Suez workers was rudimentary, and much of the work had to be done by hand. Moreover, the Suez Canal was more than twice as long as the route across Panama. Despite the differences between the two waterways, the success of the Suez Canal signaled that a canal across Panama was possible.

able sum regardless. The United States also promised to pay Panama another $250,000 each year as a form of rent; of course, steady inflation made this amount worth less and less as the years went by. And the unspoken promise of American protection was of some value to Panama as well. It was extremely unlikely that any foreign power would try to take over Panama while the Americans held a strong interest in the canal. Still, the contract was one-sided, and many Panamanians strenuously objected to it.

Panamanian criticism was of little importance to Americans, though. Roosevelt treated the contract as a great victory for the United States, and Congress agreed, approving the treaty easily. In fact, most segments of American society supported the notion of a canal across the isthmus. Merchants believed that a canal would increase trade and make commerce more efficient; labor leaders pointed to the jobs the canal construction would create; military officials were determined to avoid a repeat of the *Oregon* incident of 1898. To be sure, a few Americans disapproved of Roosevelt's involvement in making Panama independent. "It teaches the weaker republics of this [Western] hemisphere to distrust and fear us," complained one observer. "It lowers the moral standard of our whole people."[8] The average American, however, had no such regrets.

Designing the Canal

The treaty with Panama completed, it was now time to determine exactly what route the canal would take—and what kind of canal it would be. The first question was easy to answer: The canal would follow the basic path planned out by de Lesseps, cutting across the isthmus from Panama City on the Pacific to the city of Colón on the Caribbean Sea. The second question, however, was more difficult. There are two basic types of canals. The first of these, sometimes called a sea-level canal, can be used whenever the two bodies of water to be linked are at the same elevation. As the name suggests, a sea-level canal is built by digging down to the level of the two lakes, oceans, or seas to be connected and forming a channel between them. Sea-level canals are quite simple to construct and maintain.

The other type of canal is more complex. This type is used when the two bodies of water are not at the same elevation or where conditions make it impractical to create a sea-level canal. These canals use a system of locks to raise and lower boats as they go through the waterway. A typical lock has two gates spaced far enough apart to fit a ship between them. A ship moving from a higher elevation to a lower elevation enters the lock through an open gate at the higher end and stops when it reaches the closed gate at the front of the lock. The open gate is then closed behind the ship, and the water in the lock is gradually piped out until the ship is at the same level as the water in the lower elevation. Then the front gate opens and the ship continues on its journey. To move a ship upward, the procedure is reversed, with water entering the lock until the ship has reached the higher level.

Canals with locks are far more complicated than sea-level canals. Locks can be difficult to build and maintain, and they must be care-fully engineered to make sure the gates are watertight—and spaced an appropriate distance apart. As a result, sea-level canals are generally cheaper. They are also common. The Suez Canal, which had been completed several decades earlier, was a sea-level canal, and the French had intended to build a sea-level canal across the Panamanian isthmus. The potentially lower price tag, the success of Suez, and the example of the earlier French attempt all made some American engineers and politicians argue in favor of digging a sea-level canal through Panama.

The notion of a sea-level canal, however, also had a significant disadvantage: Panama's terrain. Unlike the flat deserts that surround the Suez Canal in the Middle East, Panama is hilly and sometimes mountainous, and digging down to sea level represented a major undertaking. Although engineers generally believed that a sea-level canal

How the Panama Canal Locks Work

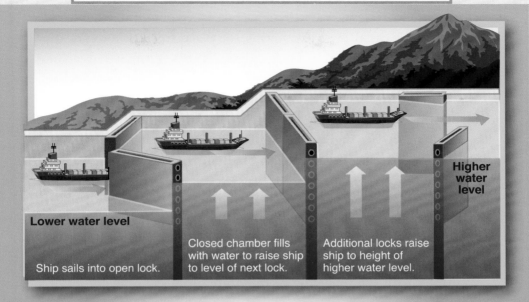

Lower water level

Higher water level

Ship sails into open lock.

Closed chamber fills with water to raise ship to level of next lock.

Additional locks raise ship to height of higher water level.

Source: How Stuff Works, "How the Panama Canal Works." www.geography.howstuffworks.com.

could in fact be built, most worried that moving that much soil would be extremely difficult. Thus, a sea-level canal would be both expensive and time-consuming. Roosevelt, moreover, had made it clear that time was of the essence. "Make the dirt fly,"[9] he instructed members of the commission charged with carrying out the canal construction.

The commission soon found itself leaning in the direction of building a canal with locks rather than one without. "If to adopt the plan of a sea-level canal means to incur great hazard and to insure indefinite delay," read an engineering report, "then [a sea-level canal] is not preferable. . . . The delay in transit of the vessels owing to additional locks would be of small consequence when compared with shortening the time for the construction of the canal or diminishing the risks in the construction."[10] In 1905—after construction had begun on the two ends of the canal—chief engineer John Stevens made the final decision: The canal would include locks.

Final Details

With his fellow engineers, Stevens also sketched out some other details regarding the canal. A ship entering the canal from either end, they decided, would be lifted in three steps or stages, ultimately reaching an elevation of 85 feet (26 m) above sea level, and then lowered back to sea level using three more sets of locks. Throughout its length the canal would be wide enough to allow two relatively large ships to pass one another. At the highest elevation a dam across a major river would flood 164 square miles (425 sq. km) of countryside and create a large lake, to be known as Gatun Lake. This lake would double as the center of the canal, accounting in all for about half the canal's total distance. The engineers also needed to construct breakwaters and other devices to shield the entrances to the canal from storms and strong currents, which were especially prevalent off Panama's Pacific shoreline.

Along with the finalizing of the route came the drawing up of a budget. The engineers estimated that the total cost of the canal would come to $375 million—an even more enormous sum at the time than it is today, but one that suited such an enormous project. Of that figure, $10 million had already been paid to Panama and another $40 million to the French, so the construction itself was expected to cost about $325 million—or more than three times the cost of the entire Suez Canal several decades earlier. According to the estimates, the Panama Canal would be the most expensive construction project in American history, and the price tag gave some observers pause. But Roosevelt was not deterred. Instead, he rejoiced in the completion of the plan. The Panama Canal, he predicted, would be "the great bit of work of my administration, and from the material and constructive standpoint one of the greatest bits of work that the twentieth century will see."[11]

By 1905, then, the plans for the canal were more or less complete. But of course making the plans was the easy part. The main challenges still lay ahead. Cutting through the hills, creating Gatun Lake, constructing the locks, and more—all in one of the harshest environments on earth—would prove extremely complex. Fortunately, the people who planned and constructed the canal were up to the task.

CHAPTER TWO

Construction

F ew construction projects of the early 1900s approached the scope and complexity of the Panama Canal. Building the canal required thousands of workers to dig out millions upon millions of cubic yards of rock, soil, and other material; construct elaborate dams, breakwaters, and locks; and transport men, materials, and equipment up and down the isthmus. The completion of the canal—on time and under budget—was a testament to the hard work and dedication of the people involved in the project. Few projects of similar size, then or now, have been carried out with such focus, organization, and skill. "It is the greatest task of its . . . kind that has ever been performed,"[12] wrote Theodore Roosevelt in his autobiography, and his argument is hard to dispute.

The Labor Force

Roosevelt quickly named a group of engineers, military personnel, and other leaders to oversee the construction of the canal. Among the first tasks of these administrators was to find workers. The scale of the project called for thousands of workers to fill an enormous variety of jobs. The best-paid and best-respected among these workers held white-collar posts; these included accountants, engineers, and planners, among others. These were the men—and they were virtually all men—who made sure the project stayed on schedule, made sure the best possible equipment was sent to Panama in a timely fashion, and oversaw the spending that made the canal building possible. Most of the people who held these jobs were well-educated Americans, nearly all of them white, who were attracted to Panama for the opportunity to be involved in a new and interesting project—and in the hope of rising swiftly through the corporate or government ranks to jobs that would carry even more prestige and an even higher salary in the future.

The number of white-collar workers, however, was dwarfed by the number of skilled blue-collar laborers needed for the project. Building the Panama Canal required people to drive railroad cars, cut sheet metal, repair steam shovels, and much more. One published list of skilled laborers needed for construction work included "Iron Workers, Steam Shovel Engineers, Steam Shovel Crane Operators, Molders, Painters, Pipefitters, Tinsmiths,"[13] and many more. By far the majority of the people who held these jobs were Americans, and just as with the white-collar workers, almost all of the skilled laborers were white. Though some of these men learned on the job, the skilled laborers who helped build the Panama Canal generally arrived on the isthmus well versed in their trades, and most had several years of work experience as well.

The third, and largest, class of workers was made up of unskilled laborers. Unlike the skilled workers, these men were largely brought in from countries outside the United States. With the exception of some men who came from Italy, Croatia, and other areas in southern and eastern Europe, they would be identified today as Hispanic, black, or both. The bulk of them came from the Caribbean islands of Jamaica and Barbados. Indeed, canal officials recruited heavily in these islands, and a steady stream of workers from Jamaica and elsewhere arrived in the Canal Zone throughout the years of canal construction—as many as a thousand at a time. The work ethic of these islanders was much admired by the officials in charge of the canal. Barbadians, in particular, "find employment almost immediately with the Commission," the Canal

WORDS IN CONTEXT
breakwaters
Concrete barriers that protect harbors.

Men dig a miniature canal to drain water from Gatun Lake. Thousands of unskilled workers were required to help build the Panama Canal.

Zone newspaper, known as the *Canal Record*, reported, "and prove to be good workmen."[14]

Whether they came from Jamaica, Nicaragua, or Greece, the unskilled laborers hired to build the canal worked menial jobs that usually involved heavy lifting. Many of them spent their days digging with shovels, laying railroad track, hacking at the dense undergrowth in the rain forests of the isthmus, or loading and unloading earth from train cars. The work was dull, repetitive, and hard, and by American standards the laborers were not well paid. Nonetheless, working on the canal represented an improvement for many laborers. Most came from places where poverty was widespread, unemployment was common, and workers had few if any rights. Though Panama was scarcely a paradise, for most laborers working and living conditions on the isthmus were generally better than they were back home.

Surveys and Excavation

The process of building the canal began with surveying the route the waterway would take. Some of this work had already been done by the French; still, surveyors had to check that the French data was still valid and also had to make charts of areas the French had not yet reached. By surveying the countryside, the workers determined accurate distances between points along the canal route. They also made certain that they knew the elevations of the various places through which the completed canal would pass. Precision was critical; even a small error in a survey could cause serious complications as the work continued.

Once an area had been surveyed, workers dug down to the appropriate elevation. That required a number of steps. First, crews removed trees, bushes, and other plants along the canal's path in the densely forested isthmus, laying the ground bare. In relatively flat areas, workers could then use mechanical shovels or hand shovels to scoop layers of soil off the ground. That was especially possible where the surface was made up primarily of dirt or mud with few large rocks mixed in. Even then, however, the work was not easy or pleasant. The labor of shoveling by hand was backbreaking, steam shovels had an unfortunate tendency to break down while on the job, and workers often had to do their jobs while knee-deep in mud or standing water.

WORDS IN CONTEXT
clefts
Narrow, deep spaces.

Leveling relatively flat and smooth territory, however, was considerably easier than dealing with rocks. Pulling rocks out of the ground, even with heavy machinery, could be complicated. Mechanical shovels of the time could dislodge rocks that weighed more than 20,000 pounds (9,070 kg). Unfortunately, handling such a heavy load put them at high risk of breaking. Moreover, the number of steam shovels on the isthmus was limited; in July 1907, for instance, the canal commission had fewer than sixty-five mechanical shovels actually in service. To move larger rocks, then, or to move less weighty rocks when steam shovels were not available, workers used dynamite to blast the stones into smaller pieces.

⬡ GEORGE GOETHALS

Theodore Roosevelt was responsible for getting the Panama Canal started. Roosevelt's enthusiasm for building a waterway across Central America, coupled with his political maneuvering to split Panama from Colombia, made the canal a real possibility. But for all his hard work, Roosevelt was not the pivotal figure in the history of the canal. That honor belongs instead to George Goethals, a civil engineer and army officer who supervised the building of the canal from 1907 until its completion in 1914.

A graduate of West Point, Goethals began his engineering career soon after finishing school. Among his first projects was the construction of a bridge across the Spokane River in Washington. Later he supervised the construction of the Muscle Shoals Canal in Alabama—a project for which he designed the tallest canal lock ever used to that time. In 1907 he replaced John Stevens as head of the Panama Canal project. In keeping with his army background, Goethals saw the work on the canal in military terms. "I now consider that I am commanding the Army of Panama," Goethals explained, "and the enemy we are going to combat is the Culebra Cut and the locks and dams at both ends of the canal."

Though he could be harsh and occasionally arrogant, Goethals was generally well respected by the workers under his command. And there is no disputing his success in pushing the project to completion. He unquestionably deserves his nickname: "The Genius of the Panama Canal."

Quoted in American Experience, "The Chief Engineers of the Panama Canal," PBS.org. www .pbs.org.

The Culebra Cut

Even more challenging was the process of cutting a route through a hillside. Again and again, laborers were required to flatten hills or expand a narrow valley between two steep slopes. Although it was rare for workers to have to remove more than about 200 vertical feet (61 m) or so of earth to reach the appropriate elevation, even digging up half that amount was extremely laborious. By far the most difficult problem faced by the workers in this regard was a 9-mile (14.5 km) stretch known as the Culebra Cut. (It has also been called the Gaillard Cut, after the man who was primarily in charge of excavating it.) The Culebra Cut featured rocky hills reaching more than 300 feet (91 m) high that had to be reduced to a height of about 45 feet (13.7 m)—no easy task.

The Culebra Cut was especially tricky because cutting the earth out of the hillsides created deep clefts with high, nearly vertical walls. These walls were often unstable, and they were prone to tumbling down. The *Canal Record* regularly reported on these avalanches, or "slides" as they were frequently called. "Thirteen slides were in motion in the territory of the Central Division [that is, at or near the Culebra Cut] during the fiscal year 1909," the newspaper noted. In general, officials minimized the disruption of the slides on the construction of the canal. "None of the slides has proved of serious detriment to the work,"[15] the *Record* took pains to explain, pointing out that most slides were quite small and that far more material was being pulled out of the excavation sites than was falling into them.

The *Record*'s contentions were no doubt true. Still, there is no question that the regular avalanches caused problems. It was surely frustrating for the workers to see so much of their hard work ruined when the walls of the cuts fell in: Even if the amount of earth crashing to the bottom of the cut was relatively small, it still added to the material that needed to be excavated. To make matters worse, the slides often covered steam shovels and other machinery, which had to be dug out again before work could proceed. Similarly, sometimes a slide could carry equipment several hundred feet from its original position, requiring workers to return the equipment to its proper place before continuing the excavation.

Transportation

The enormous amounts of earth produced in the digging represented a problem as well. As author Jeremy Sherman Snapp puts it, "Removing millions of cubic yards of dirt and rock was not so much an exca-

The nine-mile Culebra Cut (pictured) was one of the most challenging projects in the process of building the Panama Canal. Unstable cliff walls led to many avalanches, or slides.

vation challenge as a transportation problem."[16] From early on, fortunately, canal officials had a clear idea of how to handle this issue. They had laborers lay railroad tracks leading from the worksites to the cities at either end of the canal's route. As excavation of a given area began, dozens of empty railroad cars, known as dump cars, stood along the tracks waiting to be filled with earth displaced from the digging. Up to about twenty dump cars were grouped into a train, each pulled by an engine equipped with a coal car that could carry 40 to 50 tons (36.3 to 45.4 metric tons) of fuel.

The process was quick and efficient. As the laborers dislodged soil and rock, engineers maneuvered the trains into position so the dump cars could be filled with the rubble. Workers then used steam shovels to transfer the debris into the cars. Once all the cars in a train were full, a process that could take less than an hour if all went well, the engineer guided the train away from the work area, and another set of

THE CULEBRA CUT

As construction on the Panama Canal continued, eyewitnesses to the work going on at the Culebra Cut were particularly impressed by what they saw. An American visitor named Albert Edwards wrote the following in about 1910.

> It is as busy a place as an anthill. It seems to be alive with machinery; there are, of course, men in the cut too, but they are insignificant, lost among the mechanical monsters which are jerking work-trains about the maze of tracks, which are boring holes for the blasting, which are tearing at the spine of the continent—steam shovels which fill a car in five moves, steam shovels as accurate and delicate as a watch, as mighty—Well, I can think of nothing sufficiently mighty to compare with these steel beasts which eat a thousand cubic yards a day out of the side of the hills.
>
> But it is not till you get beyond the cut and, looking back, see the profile of the ditch against the sunset that you get the real impression—the memory which is to last. The scars on the side of the cut are red, like the rocks of our great Western deserts. The work has stopped, and the great black shovels are silhouetted against the red of the sky. Then there comes a moment, as your train winds round a curve, when the lowering sun falls directly into the notch of the cut and it is all illumined in an utterly unearthly glory.

Albert Edwards, "A Look at Panama," *Outlook*, vol. 94, 1910, p. 32.

empty dump cars took its place. The trains came and went with great dispatch, and observers were impressed with the number of trains moving around the isthmus. So, for that matter, were the locals. "The number of trains passing a given point on a single day has been as many [as] 196,"[17] the *Canal Record* marveled in 1907; and although a more common figure was 150 trains per day, even that number still represented a notable achievement.

What happened to the debris varied. Some of it was simply dumped into the ocean. More was used to build up the banks of the canal. Perhaps the bulk of it, however, went to build Gatun Dam, an earthen dam placed across the Chagres River in the center of the isthmus. This dam eventually created Gatun Lake, which made up an important stretch of the canal and provided much of the water needed for the locks' operation. When Gatun Dam was built, it was by a considerable margin the largest earthen dam ever constructed. Measuring 1.5 miles (2.4 km) in length, the dam is about 1,700 feet (518 m) thick. Given that size, it made perfect sense to make the bulk of the dam out of materials excavated by the diggers elsewhere along the canal's route.

Once the trains bound for the Gatun Dam region arrived at their destination, laborers using steam shovels unloaded the trains and used the materials inside the dump cars to build the dam. They began at either side of the river and worked their way slowly toward the center. Construction also relied on hydraulic pumps, which suctioned up rock and other material from the bottom of the Chagres and added it to the dam as it was put together. Still, constructing the dam would have been much more difficult if not for the reuse of the materials carved from the hillsides and brought by train to the site of the dam. Over a period of seven years, workers moved 96 million cubic yards (73.4 million cu. m) of earth out of the Culebra Cut—much of it going to form the massive Gatun Dam.

> **WORDS IN CONTEXT**
> hydraulic
> *Operated by the pressure of moving water.*

Dredging

The removal of material from under the water was not limited to the area immediately surrounding Gatun Dam. To make the canal fully accessible to ships, it was often necessary for workers to remove rock and earth from river bottoms and the ocean floor. This process, known as dredging, was especially common in Gatun Lake and in both approaches to the canal. Limon Bay, a large but shallow body of water near the city of Colón on the canal's Atlantic side, was particularly in need of dredging. In September 1909 alone, the *Canal Record* reported, workers dredged about 650,000 cubic yards (496,960 cu. m) of material from the bay.

The approach to the canal's Pacific terminus also required extensive dredging. For various reasons, mostly due to political wrangling about the site of one of the locks, this work was delayed for a number of months. By 1909, however, work had commenced, and dredging was well under way along Panama's Pacific coastline. At one point during that year, thirty-four different dredges—ships that looked something like barges—were working in the Pacific. One of the largest of these, the *Culebra*, could suction up 15,000 cubic yards (11,468 cu. m) in a single day. "She toiled 24 hours a day, six days a week," writes Snapp, "and on Sundays her coal bunkers were filled . . . and maintenance work was performed."[18]

Dredges on the isthmus came in several different sizes and types. Where the river or ocean floor consisted mainly of gravel or mud, suction dredges worked especially well. Clay, larger rocks, and packed earth, on the other hand, tended to yield more easily to scoops than to suction; the most common scoop was a type of grabber known as a clamshell. The most complicated dredging task, however, involved bodies of water with heavy rock at the bottom. The canal commission used ships called drill barges in these situations. Drill barges had machinery designed to drill some distance into the rock. Workers would then drop dynamite charges into the holes and detonate them, causing the rock to break apart. In extreme cases the rock could be pulverized by using a special drill that rammed the stone repeatedly.

Building the Locks

The final stage of building the canal was constructing the locks. The first step in this process was to build dams that would temporarily keep away the water from oceans and rivers—a necessity, since it was not feasible to build a lock underwater. Like the big dam that formed Gatun Lake, these dams were largely made of earth. And though these dams were not nearly as large as the Gatun Dam, they took plenty of time and effort to construct. One of these dams, built at Pedro Miguel on the Pacific side of the canal, was 1,400 feet (427 m) long and 40 feet (12 m) wide at its narrowest point. Once in place, the dams kept water from flowing into the lock area, making construction of the locks possible.

By any standard—but particularly compared to other structures of the early twentieth century—the locks were massive. Not only did the locks need to be long enough and wide enough to hold a ship while the water level around it changed, but they needed to be tall as well. Each lock chamber measures more than 1,000 feet (305 m) long and about 110 feet (34 m) wide. But because there are two lanes for each lock, and because the walls of the lock need to be strong and thick, the actual width of the locks is closer to 375 feet (114 m). And the height of the lock gates, while not consistent from one set of locks to the next, averages about 200 feet (61 m).

The sheer size of the locks, then, required enormous amounts of concrete and steel. Workers needed about 4.5 million cubic yards (3.4 million cu. m) of concrete—more than would be used for any other project until the construction of Hoover Dam in the early 1930s. The concrete was a mix of cement, water, sand, and gravel, much of it obtained from the dredging and excavation elsewhere along the isthmus. Like other materials dug up in the process of building the canal, the gravel and sand were shipped to the lock sites by railroad. Massive cranes—some of them up to 62 feet (19 m) tall and weighing 470 tons (426 metric tons)—did the mixing. Other cranes dumped the concrete inside steel forms placed where the locks would eventually go; the forms gave the concrete the proper shape while it dried.

Workers built the locks slowly and carefully. Measurements needed to be precise; even a small measuring error could make the lock inoperable. "The plates [part of the gates] were so exactly aligned," read an article in a 1913 edition of the *Canal Record*, when

The locks of the Panama Canal were built last. The first step in building the locks was to build a dam to prevent water from entering the area. A recent view of the canal and locks is shown.

the locks were being completed, "that the deviation from exact correctness nowhere exceeded five-thousandths of an inch."[19] Likewise, the walls, floors, and gates of the locks had to be strong and well built. As with imprecise measurement, a weak wall or a poorly constructed gate would render a lock useless.

Success

By early 1914, after a process lasting about four years, the locks were nearing completion. "The small remaining force at work at Miraflores Locks was withdrawn on January 22,"[20] reported the *Canal Record*, adding that in some other areas of construction the number of laborers had dwindled to as few as nine. By this time nearly everything else was done: The dredging was complete, Gatun Lake had been filled, and even the Culebra Cut held sufficient water to hold ships passing by. Workers now dynamited the earthen dams that protected the lock construction sites, allowing water to rush in from the oceans and from Gatun Lake in the center of the isthmus. Engineers checked and double-checked that the gates of the locks opened smoothly and closed effectively. Everything seemed in fine working order.

On August 3, 1914, a steamship called the *Cristobal* made a test trip along the canal. It was the builders' first opportunity to see how the canal would handle an actual ship, and for the most part they were pleased. "The voyage was without operating incident," the *Canal Record* announced, "other than some minor difficulties . . . at Gatun and Pedro Miguel Locks."[21] The journey took almost twelve hours, but the return trip scheduled for the next day was shorter and smoother. The remaining kinks were quickly worked out; and less than two weeks later, on August 15, a ship called the *Ancon* made the first official passage through the canal. "The dream of the centuries has become a reality," wrote Lindley Garrison, US Secretary of War, in a telegram to George Goethals, the engineer in charge of the construction. "The fully earned and deserved congratulations of a grateful people go out to you and your colaborers."[22] Ten years of intensive labor by thousands of workers had paid off. The canal was open.

CHAPTER THREE

The Workers

For many of the workers who built the Panama Canal, the Canal Zone was a difficult place to be. The labor was frequently backbreaking and sometimes dangerous. Most workers were stationed far from friends, family, and home. The Panamanian climate was inhospitable, the terrain rugged. Injuries and illness were common. So too was racism, which made life complicated and often miserable for people of African descent. As much as they could, the people hired to work on the canal made the best of a difficult situation. Still, life on the isthmus could be brutal, and the reminiscences of workers—particularly those who were unskilled laborers—were not generally positive. As one worker recalled years later about working on the canal, "I tell you it was no bed of roses."[23]

Weather and Climate

Perhaps the most noticeable problem with Panama, particularly for workers accustomed to the temperate climates of the United States, was the weather. By American standards, temperatures in Panama are extremely high. The average annual temperature in the seaside cities hovers around 80°F (27°C), but temperatures of up to 100°F (38°C) are far from unusual in the interior. Combined with high humidity levels and frequent rainfall—a whopping 237 inches (6 m) of precipitation fell on one part of the Culebra Cut in 1909—the elevated temperatures made working outdoors feel like working in a steam bath. However, workers were required to keep going regardless of the weather conditions. One hotel employee later recalled changing his suit three times a day, so heavily did he sweat in the tropical conditions.

Panama's climate created other problems, too. The combination of heat, humidity, and rainfall was highly conducive to plant growth. The interior of the isthmus, in particular, was thick with vegetation, most of which had to be removed before workers could begin digging into the soil below it. Axes, knives, and machetes were necessary equipment for the unskilled laborers assigned to prepare the land for digging. Not only was the vegetation difficult to remove, but the heavy, tangled overgrowth made moving across the countryside troublesome as well.

> **WORDS IN CONTEXT**
> machetes
> *Long knives used for chopping vegetation.*

In addition, the rain forest of the Panamanian isthmus was filled with animal life, some of which presented a hazard to humans. Jaguars, the largest members of the cat family native to the Western Hemisphere, prowled swamps and forests looking for prey. Snakes, some of them poisonous, bit unsuspecting men. The mere possibility of encountering these or similar tropical creatures was enough to unnerve many workers. Even towns and cities were no refuge from snakes, which were happy to slither almost anywhere on the isthmus, and rats were extremely common in built-up areas.

Fever and Mosquitoes

The most dangerous animals in Panama, however, were far smaller than even the tiniest snakes or cats. These were mosquitoes that carried serious and often fatal diseases such as yellow fever and malaria. Being bitten by an infected mosquito almost always resulted in a week or more of utter misery, marked by symptoms such as high fevers, intense vomiting, violent shaking, and temporary insanity. "In about ten days from now," ran a surprisingly lighthearted verse about yellow fever published in 1905,

Iron bands will clamp your brow
. . . Your mouth will taste of untold things
With claws and horns and fins and wings.
Your head will weigh a ton or more,
And forty gales within it roar![24]

But malaria and yellow fever were no laughing matter. Tens of thousands of people in Panama, including those working at desk jobs and those who labored in the outdoor rain forests, were affected by mosquito-borne diseases during the early years of digging the canal. In the first year of canal construction, in particular, more than 80 percent of the workers contracted one or the other of these diseases. Many died. Most workers in those early years lived in constant fear of becoming sick, and it did not take much to get them to hop onto a ship that would take them back to their homelands—or almost anywhere else. "Even a whisper of an outbreak sent boatloads of men fleeing,"[25] notes a website.

As time went on and scientists became more aware of the mechanism by which the diseases were spread, efforts to control malaria and yellow fever increasingly concentrated on controlling the mosquito population on the isthmus. Residents were cautioned to eliminate standing water, where mosquitoes were likely to breed, and to use screens and mosquito netting, when possible, to protect themselves as they worked, played, and slept. The measures were highly effective. "The last case [of yellow fever] which originated in the Zone was in May, 1906,"[26] boasted the *Canal Record* in 1908; and though malaria proved more difficult to eradicate, its incidence was reduced considerably as people followed the directions of the canal authorities.

While yellow fever and malaria were the most feared diseases in Panama, they were not the only ones bringing terror to the people on the isthmus. Cases of the bubonic plague, for example, were occasionally reported in the Canal Zone. Most of these cases were brought into

WORDS IN CONTEXT
eradicate
To eliminate or get rid of.

Malaria and yellow fever plagued the Panama Canal workers. Many workers contracted these diseases and many died from them before scientists understood that the diseases were carried by mosquitoes.

Central America by sailors arriving on ships from infected ports in South America and elsewhere. Health officials did their best to combat the plague by exterminating rats (believed to carry the plague) wherever they could be found and by placing ill sailors in quarantine until it could be determined whether they actually had the disease. Typhoid fever, spread largely by drinking contaminated water, was another problem for residents of Panama during the years of canal construction.

YELLOW FEVER AND MOSQUITOES

Until shortly before construction began on the Panama Canal, no one knew what caused tropical diseases like malaria and yellow fever. The most common theory was that these diseases were caused by miasma—bad or poisoned air. Others argued that the ailments were caused by eating infected bananas, oranges, and other foods native to the tropics. Most believed, moreover, that the diseases could be transferred from one person to another via infected clothing, bedding, and utensils.

Through the efforts of several creative scientists, however, it gradually became clear that the true culprit was the mosquito. Among the first to postulate this theory was an American doctor named Walter Reed. Reed advocated fighting malaria and yellow fever by installing mosquito-proof screens, exterminating mosquitoes when possible, and making it difficult for mosquitoes to breed.

Although Reed had plenty of evidence to support his contention, not everyone accepted his conclusions. Among these was J.G. Walker, an American admiral stationed in Panama early in the construction process. Walker was furious when the federal government assigned a doctor named William Gorgas to try to control mosquitoes on the isthmus. "I am not going to spend good American dollars," Walker complained, "on a group of insane enthusiasts who spend their time chasing mosquitoes!" Fortunately, Walker was soon replaced by a more forward-thinking engineer named John Stevens, who provided Gorgas with plenty of funding and support. Before long, mosquito-borne disease had been greatly reduced in the Canal Zone.

Quoted in Jean West, "Dr. Gorgas Defeats 'Yellow Jack,'" *Cobblestone*, April 2001, p. 20.

Accidental Death

Death along the canal did not come from only mosquitoes and rats. The heavy machinery used to build the canal was dangerous, and accidents were frequent. Trains derailed, injuring or killing those riding inside—or those working along the tracks. The engines of steam shovels and cranes overheated and blew up, killing anyone standing nearby. Even when heavy equipment was not involved, worksites were treacherous. Men fell between the timbers of trestles, were crushed by landslides, drowned in culverts when sandbag barriers were washed away by powerful currents, and died of electric shock when touching wires that had not been properly grounded. "I feel blessed to be still alive,"[27] one worker reported after leaving the isthmus.

Of all the accidents that took place along the canal, dynamite was probably responsible for the greatest number. Workers could not completely control when and where dynamite charges would go off. All too often, the explosives detonated as they were being placed, with horrible consequences for the workers holding the material. Other times the fuses on the dynamite went off early, killing or maiming those who had not been able to retreat in time. "In an explosion of dynamite," reported the *Canal Record* in 1909—one of many similar announcements through the years of construction— "four men were killed and nine were injured."[28] The dangers of dynamite mainly affected the "powder men" who were responsible for measuring out charges, setting them in place, and lighting the fuses, but other workers could be killed by explosives as well. In 1913, for instance, a Jamaican carpenter was killed by a rock carried through the air by a dynamite blast.

The combination of fever and accidents led to an extremely high death rate among canal workers, especially in the early days of construction. Even by 1907, when yellow fever had been wiped out, the mortality rate among unskilled workers was forty-two per thousand— substantially higher than death rates for similar populations today. Death was a constant concern for many of the people who worked on the canal. "You had to pray every day for God to carry you safe," one worker remembered. "Those were the times you go to bed at nights and the next day you may be a dead man."[29] It was said that the number of deaths among workers building the canal was equal to the number of railroad ties laid during the course of construction, and while this was an exaggeration, thousands of men did indeed die while on the job.

Life on the Isthmus

But the increased chance of death was not the only problem with Panama. Living conditions on the isthmus, in general, were far from ideal. For many workers, much of the issue was simply that Panama did not match their expectations. "A great many of the young men who come to the Isthmus have been moved by a spirit of adventure," noted one official. "Arriving here, and surrounded as they are by the conditions that exist, without diversions, without home influences, and especially without the influences of wives, mothers, and sisters, they become discontented and homesick."[30] Many of these workers, disappointed by the realities of life far from family and friends, left for home as soon as they could.

And many of those who stayed had legitimate complaints about life on the isthmus. The issues were especially apparent in the case of the unskilled laborers who worked on the canal, most notably among those who came to Panama from Barbados, Jamaica, and elsewhere in the West Indies. Known as "silver employees," most likely because they were originally paid their wages in silver coins, they did not enjoy the rights and privileges granted to the canal's "gold employees"—the skilled laborers and managerial professionals, most of them white, who typically came from the United States. The working conditions for the silver employees were more severe than the conditions faced by gold employees, and the death rate among silver employees was three or four times higher than the corresponding rate among gold employees.

If conditions on the job were bad for silver employees, ordinary living conditions were less than pleasant as well. That was deliberate. In much of the United States during the early 1900s, people were separated by color both by law and by custom. The so-called Jim Crow laws, especially popular in the South, mandated that African Americans and whites be kept apart in theaters, hotels, schools, and much more. Accepting this discrimination as natural and sensible, the officials in

Men stand atop train wreckage after a landslide in the Culebra Cut. Such accidents were frequent occurrences.

charge of constructing the canal set up a similar system in the Canal Zone. As a result, segregation—the enforced separation of the races—was commonplace on the American-controlled parts of the isthmus. Even the post office had separate counters: one for the silver employees, another for the gold. As journalist Frederic Jennings Haskin approvingly wrote in a 1914 summary of the canal's construction, "The color line was kindly but firmly drawn throughout the work."[31]

Discrimination

Kindly was not the word that the silver employees would have used, however. The accommodations offered the silver employees were not in any way equal to those provided for the workers who qualified for gold status. As historian Julie Greene observes, "The government paid silver employees far less, fed them unappetizing food, and housed them in substandard shacks."[32] Railroad cars reserved for blacks were appallingly crowded, while whites rode in cars with plenty of space for everyone. The schools open to black children were less well equipped than those intended for the children of white employees. Even the water provided for silver employees was often foul.

For silver employees, housing was perhaps the most obvious sign of discrimination. Few silver employees lived in comfortable conditions. Most lived in small tenement houses, often without working window screens and frequently built on swampy land or on unstable land above worksites. Alternatively, the government provided barracks and packed them with as many men as would fit; in one case seventy-two men lived in a building measuring 30 feet by 50 feet (9 m by 15 m). If these accommodations were full—and they often were—new employees were forced to take up residence in empty boxcars, pitch tents on empty land, or rent rooms at their own expense in the zone's few population centers.

The silver employees generally accepted the discrimination without much obvious complaint. It helped that while wages in Panama were considerably lower for silver employees than they were for gold employees, they tended to be far higher than what these men could have earned at home. Indeed, workers from Barbados, in particular, had a reputation for showing off their newly found wealth when they returned home with their wages, meager as they were by American standards. Still, silver employees frequently chafed under the restrictive laws and customs, and emotions sometimes boiled over. In 1909, for example, violence broke out when several West Indians, fed up with the cramped conditions in a train car packed with silver employees, tried to sit in a whites-only car instead. The Canal Zone police force, set up and overseen by the American commission that administered the zone, was needed to restore order.

Attempts to change the system, however, were doomed to failure. Canal officials had no interest in listening to complaints from the West Indian workers. If one worker chose to leave because of unfair living and working conditions, there were a dozen more eager to take his place. Moreover, many white workers put pressure on canal leadership to maintain discriminatory practices. "We do not feel inclined to work on a level basis with a negro,"[33] one white employee explained, and it seems clear that most gold employees agreed. Afraid that black workers might take their jobs, depress wages, and infringe on their own special privileges, most white Americans working in the Canal Zone did what they could to keep the distinction between gold and silver employees alive.

WOMEN WORKERS

Given the beliefs about men's and women's roles common in American society at the beginning of the twentieth century, it is not surprising that women played no direct role in the construction of the Panama Canal. The project required a large support staff, however, and a few of the workers who filled these roles were women. Some served as teachers in Canal Zone schools, others as secretaries and clerks. The majority of women in the workforce, though, were nurses who were assigned to one of the two main hospitals in the zone.

Many of these positions were filled by drawing from the wives and daughters of men already employed by the canal, but some intrepid women paid their own way to Panama to look for work. Some craved adventure; others had heard that wages were higher in Panama than in most of the United States. Some found what they were looking for. Historian Julie Greene writes of nurses, in particular, who felt empowered by working in hospitals where women collectively wielded a fair amount of authority. But others found the experience frustrating. The wages offered female workers were considerably lower than the wages offered to men doing similar work. And quite often job offers were not extended to women at all. "Aliens, sots [drunkards], sharpers [gamblers], any old thing, will be given a position in an office by the Isthmian Canal Commission," complained a stenographer named Mary Chatfield, "anything but an American woman."

Quoted in Julie Greene, *The Canal Builders*. New York: Penguin, 2009, p. 109.

Gold Employees

Where canal officials saw the silver employees as more or less inter-changeable, they did not feel the same way about the gold employees. On the contrary, in the early days of canal construction officials were deeply worried about high turnover among managerial employees and skilled laborers: In 1905 about 75 percent of American workers left Panama after just a few months. Rather than trying to train West Indians or Central Americans to take on these positions, the govern-ment chose instead to make life in the Canal Zone as appealing as possible to American workers in hopes that they would stay.

Pay was one way in which canal officials sought to show American workers that they were valued. While unskilled West Indian labor-ers might earn a dollar a day, a skilled white American worker could earn $150 or even $200 a month, and educated workers with desk jobs routinely earned double that. Time off was another incentive.

The typical worker's camp (pictured) was often built on swampland. Most housing had no window screens, and offered little protection from insects and the elements.

With airplane flight still in its infancy and the closest American ports more than 1,000 miles (1,609 km) away, travel to and from the United States required plenty of time, and gold employees typically received a six-week vacation each year. They also got thirty days of sick leave—a benefit denied altogether to most silver employees.

Housing was yet another way to reward gold employees. Gold workers were encouraged to bring their families to Panama; each family was housed in a comfortable two-story private house at government expense. Basic furnishings for each house were also provided without cost to the employee; this list included dining and kitchen tables, three rocking chairs, a bed with mattress and pillows, and a refrigerator. The best-paid workers were also entitled to a porch swing, a desk, and a towel rack, among other perks. Many observers were impressed by the quality of the houses and their furnishings. The Americans, wrote English traveler Winifred James, made Panama "blossom immediately with all the products of the most modern civilization."[34]

Clubs, Music, and Baseball

To further make gold employees feel at home on the isthmus, canal officials also assisted in introducing American amusements and customs into the Canal Zone. In an era when many professional American men belonged to fraternal organizations, for example, the Americans who lived in Panama formed clubs similar to those they had known back home in Virginia, Texas, or Indiana. These included the Masons, the Improved Order of Red Men, and the Independent Order of Panamanian Kangaroos. The organizations were supposedly service clubs with similar goals and ideals, but they did not always act in tandem with one another. In fact, the groups took pride in their separate identities and were careful to remain distinct from one another. "This will be strictly a Kangaroo dance," read a news item in the *Canal Record*, "and others are requested not to present themselves."[35]

With entire families moving to the Canal Zone, women's clubs were popular on the isthmus as well. In every city and town, women joined together to learn about art and music, carry out civic improvements, or simply socialize. Several, noting that Spanish was extremely useful in Panama but rarely spoken by newcomers to the isthmus, offered Spanish lessons to Americans. Others set up lending libraries. In addition to the service orientation, the mere existence of the clubs was a blessing to many women who found themselves isolated in a strange new country. "Until women's clubs were started in the Zone," reported one veteran of the Canal Zone in 1908, "except for an occasional dance at one of the men's clubs . . . , there was absolutely nothing for a woman to do outside of her own home."[36]

Many of the clubs, men's and women's alike, sponsored cultural events. Concerts were common, with bands, string quartets, and solo singers performing a mix of classical, church, and popular music. Sports and games were extremely popular, too. Girls participated in basketball, bowling, and field hockey; results of chess tournaments were routinely reported in the *Canal Record*. No activity was as exciting to the Americans of the Canal Zone, however, as baseball. In the constantly warm weather of Panama, there was no off-season, and teams played year-round. "A team has been organized at Culebra," read a report in the *Canal Record*, "consisting entirely of players from the state of Georgia. They are open for challenges from any baseball club consisting of members from any one state in the Union and would like to get a game at an early date."[37] So popular was baseball, in fact, that athletes in the Canal Zone successfully lobbied the Isthmian Canal Commission—the governing body of the Canal Zone— to exempt baseball from a requirement that organized entertainments be subject to a five-dollar license fee.

Unfortunately, these activities were aimed at—and limited to— the gold employees. As with the benefits of excellent pay, liberal vacation time, and comfortable housing, organized baseball leagues, service clubs, and concerts were strictly for the benefit of white Americans. In trying to keep the Americans happy, canal officials widened the social and economic gap between the gold and silver employees. For all kinds of reasons, life was already hard for laborers in Panama. The commission's failure to treat the silver employees with respect simply made it worse.

CHAPTER FOUR

Transition

American officials had hoped that the canal would be an overwhelming success as soon as it opened. That was not quite the case. Partly because of World War I, which broke out just a few weeks before the *Ancon* made the first official traverse of the canal, and partly because of occasional slides that continued to block the canal along the Culebra Cut even after the waterway opened, relatively few ships took advantage of the direct route through the isthmus in the first few years of operations. In 1915, for instance, just 572 ships made the trip along the canal—an average of just over three every two days. For those who had been deeply involved in the process of planning and building the canal, the low numbers were a disappointment. And since the canal made money by charging tolls, the low numbers were problematic from a financial point of view as well.

Before long, however, business began to pick up. By the early 1920s the war was over, prosperity reigned across much of the world, and the problems at the Culebra Cut had been solved. Ships were now passing regularly through the waterway's locks, their captains deeply appreciative of having avoided the long slog around Cape Horn. "Traffic through the Canal has shown a consistent increase," the *Canal Record* noted approvingly in 1923. "The past year has been by far the best of all."[38] Indeed, the average number of ships traversing the canal was rising steadily. In the first decade of operation, statistics show

> **WORDS IN CONTEXT**
> prosperity
> *Wealth, especially in a society.*

that about 25,000 ships had gone through the canal—making for an annual average far above the 572 that had made the trip back in 1915.

But though the canal became a clear success in the decades following the *Ancon*'s inaugural run, the real story of the canal in the twentieth century was not about increased traffic. Nor was it about the headaches of keeping the locks in good working order and making sure that the shipping channels were deep enough to transport some of the world's largest ships. Instead, the story of the Panama Canal between 1914 and 2000 is primarily a story of political conflict. In particular, it is the tale of disputes, growing more intense with time, between the government and people of Panama on the one hand and those of the United States on the other.

The Cocoa Grove Incident

Conflicts between Panama and the United States had begun almost as soon as the canal was started. Toward the end of the construction process, in fact, there were several high-profile clashes between Panamanians and Americans in and around the Canal Zone. Chief among these was an altercation on July 4, 1912, when a large group of American workers enthusiastically celebrating Independence Day descended on the saloons and brothels of Cocoa Grove, the entertainment district of Panama City. Loud and boisterous to begin with, the crowd grew violent and more and more difficult to control as the night wore on. Panamanian police eventually swept in to disband the revelers and make a few arrests, but many Americans, unwilling to submit to Panamanian law and order, resisted. In the resulting chaos one American was killed and several others were badly wounded.

Panamanians and Americans interpreted the Cocoa Grove affair from very different perspectives. As the Americans saw it, the incident was entirely the fault of an overzealous and incompetent Panamanian police force. "The police lost their heads completely," read an official report from the US Army, "and got wild and excited in their actions. They used rifles, revolvers, and clubs more than was necessary."[39] The reaction of the Panamanians, however, was the opposite. As they saw

PILOTS

The Panama Canal makes extensive use of pilots, sailors experienced in steering a ship through the passage and the locks. When a ship arrives at the entrance, it is boarded by at least one pilot, sometimes two, who take over the responsibility for the ship as long as it remains in the canal. The pilots arrive in a small vessel at the side of the large ships and climb as many as ten flights of stairs above the water level to reach the bridge, the part of the ship from which the steering is done.

Although the captains know their ships much better than the pilots possibly could, the pilots know the canal. After making hundreds of trips back and forth across the isthmus, they are acutely aware of the potential pitfalls a ship might encounter. Accordingly, they understand exactly how much speed to use to get safely into each lock. They know where the waterway may be shallow or where currents might be unexpectedly strong, and they are skilled at passing vessels coming in the opposite direction.

For many pilots, this position is prized. "I got the best job in the world," says one pilot. "You get a lot of satisfaction once you finish, and you get to meet people [from] all around the world." As of 2014 more than 250 pilots are in active service.

Quoted in Jeffrey Kofman, "From Sea to Sea in the Panama Canal," ABC News, October 22, 2006. http://abcnews.go.com.

it, Panama City residents had been in grave danger from the drunken Americans, many of whom were armed, and the police response had been necessary to keep the community safe. Far from apologizing for the incident, many Panamanians instead sought an apology from the United States.

The Cocoa Grove incident was eventually resolved—but only to the satisfaction of one side. US officials completely dismissed the testimony of Panamanian policemen, along with the accounts of Panamanians who said they had been injured by the mob. The Americans alleged that these stories were blatant lies obtained through threats

Gatun Lake rises, flooding a lakeside village. Many native Panamanians lost their homes through flooding and forced relocation.

and bribery. They also dismissed the notion that the revelers presented any kind of problem. The workers who were celebrating that night, one report insisted, were simply in a "frolicsome holiday spirit."[40] As punishment, the United States demanded that Panamanian police officers be stripped of their high-powered rifles. Panama's government protested, but the massive imbalance in power between the two countries meant that the Panamanians had no choice but to comply.

More Trouble

The Cocoa Grove incident, along with several other similar events, helped set the tone for relations between the United States and Panama. By the time the canal opened, Panamanians knew that they owed the United States an enormous debt. The American desire to build a canal, after all, had led directly to the founding of their nation; without the canal, there would have been no Panama. Similarly, Panamanians knew that the payments the United States was making to Panama were and would continue to be a great boon to the young country's economy. Finally, Panama was benefiting enormously from

American know-how and American dollars. In particular, the dangers of mosquito-borne illness had been much reduced, thanks to the work of American doctors and scientists.

At the same time, Panamanians were far from content. The canal, after all, had sliced their country in two, and the Canal Zone that surrounded the waterway belonged to the United States, not to their own nation. Panama's cities were filling up with immigrants from the West Indies and elsewhere, and these immigrants competed with Panamanians for jobs and housing. The construction of dams and the subsequent flooding of millions of acres had destroyed entire villages and forced the relocation of many Panamanian citizens. And the US refusal to listen to Panamanian concerns, as evidenced by the nation's official response following the altercation in Cocoa Grove, was a major issue for many residents of Panama.

On the whole, the Panamanians who lived and worked in the Canal Zone did not feel they were being treated with respect by American workers or officials. Many were particularly unhappy with the division of laborers into gold and silver employees, a policy that continued into the first years of the canal's operation. With the majority of native Panamanians being considered either Indian or black, nearly all Panamanian workers on the canal were classed as silver employees. One Panamanian newspaper charged that the Americans were too focused on race and status to treat the Panamanians well. "Any American, whether from Maine or Alabama, resents being arrested or interfered with in any way by a negro policeman," the newspaper explained. "A large majority of Americans feel themselves very superior to any Panamanian."[41] Under these circumstances, Panamanians could not help but feel discontent.

That discontent erupted on a number of occasions during the decades immediately following the opening of the canal. In 1918, for instance, American oil companies took over some Panamanian land in a province to the west of the Canal Zone. Panamanian leaders protested, as did ordinary Panamanians, and there were several

WORDS IN CONTEXT
strike
A refusal to work.

outbreaks of violence. In response, the United States sent in military personnel to keep order and ensure that the companies' attempts to locate oil were not disturbed. In the end the troops stayed for two years. Scarcely had they left than they were needed again, with US Marines landing in Central America to force Panama to turn over some disputed territory to Costa Rica.

A different type of incident took place in 1919. Some silver employees negotiated an agreement with the canal commission to raise wages and improve working conditions for laborers along the canal. However, the governor of the Canal Zone, Chester Harding, refused to sign the agreement. In response, some silver employees called a strike. Harding responded, in turn, by firing any men who refused to work. Though he did eventually allow some of the men who struck to return to employment at the canal, Harding refused to allow the strike's leaders to be rehired. He made it clear, moreover, that his willingness to allow others to return was only because they had been "the victims of false advice and irresponsible leadership."[42]

Flags and Riots

For a time in the 1930s, it seemed as though tensions between the United States and Panama were softening. During the administration of Franklin Roosevelt, the two sides negotiated a new treaty. The treaty raised the Americans' annual payment to Panama to $430,000, a substantial increase from the previous $250,000. The treaty also recognized Panama's right to police the cities bordering the Canal Zone—a right not always honored by Americans in the past. Finally, the treaty forbade the United States from taking Panamanian land and property simply because it wanted to, which had happened on several previous occasions. In 1955 further revisions to the agreement boosted Panama's annual payment to nearly $2 million, required the United States to join the halves of Panama by building a bridge over the canal, and began the process of equalizing pay between American workers and those from Panama and the West Indies.

Still, problems persisted, and in the late 1950s tensions between

Surviving members of the class of 1964 gather in 2014 to commemorate the loss of student lives during the riots that year. A riot ensued when Panamanian students reacted to American flags flying in the Canal Zone.

Panama and the United States began to escalate once again. Perhaps emboldened by the concessions they had won from the United States over the previous quarter century, many Panamanians began demanding that the United States split the canal proceeds equally with Panama. Others went further: they insisted that the United States cede the entire Canal Zone—and the canal with it—to Panamanian control. As in the past, US officials largely ignored the Panamanians' demands.

This time, however, the reservoir of anger and frustration was deeper than American officials realized. The use of flags—both Panamanian and American—soon became a touchstone for protesters on both sides. In 1963, responding to Panamanian requests, the US government decreed that the flags of both nations should fly at various locations in the Canal Zone; previously, only the US flag could be found in the territory. But when Americans in the zone objected, the order was replaced by another saying that no flags should fly at all.

Then in January 1964 hundreds of American students in the Canal Zone defied the order by flying a US flag in front of their high school. When some Panamanian students heard of this, they attempted to set up a Panamanian flag beside it. A struggle ensued; though accounts differ, it seems likely that American students tried to tear the banner down and may have damaged it.

No one disputes that the result of the incident was violence. Furious about the American students' actions—and more broadly, the years of poor treatment from the United States—mobs of Panamanians stormed into the Canal Zone intent on causing trouble. Cars were overturned; houses belonging to American dignitaries were set on fire. "We had to crawl around because we were being shot at," recalled an American ambulance driver. "There were bullet holes everywhere."[43] Canal Zone police officers, unable to control the rioters, quickly enlisted the help of the US military. Even so, violence raged for several days. By the time the riot was finally over, about two dozen people—most of them Panamanian—were dead, another two hundred people had been injured, and property damage exceeded $2 million.

More Negotiation

The riots demonstrated that Panamanian citizens were deeply unhappy with the situation as it was. American control of the Canal Zone was becoming more and more offensive to natives of the isthmus. So was the rather high-handed attitude of the American government and the authorities in the Canal Zone toward Panama and its leaders. In the aftermath of the riots, even Panamanian officials who had previously been happy to leave the canal's operation in American hands began to question their thinking. Appalled by what he saw as unnecessary belligerence on the part of American soldiers, Panamanian president Roberto Chiari briefly suspended diplomatic relations between the United States and Panama and demanded that the treaty between the countries be renegotiated to give Panama a better deal.

The riots affected American leaders' view of the situation, too. President Lyndon Johnson saw the riots as a potential stumbling block to any revision of the treaty. Making concessions to the Panamanians following a violent outburst, Johnson and his advisers believed, would set a bad precedent and encourage future protesters to resort to rioting to get what they wanted as well. It did not help that public opinion among Americans in the Canal Zone was solidly against Panama's demands. In particular, American residents of the zone, afraid that their way of life would change, strongly opposed giving Panama any further responsibility for the canal, let alone giving the waterway to Panama entirely.

At the same time, however, two factors were weighing against the Americans of the zone. The first was international feeling, which following the riots was solidly on the side of the Panamanians. Both Britain and France, for instance, charged that Panama was being bullied and advised the United States to behave more generously toward the Panamanian government. Several South American countries that usually were staunch supporters of US policy, moreover, were noticeably unsupportive of the United States where Panama was concerned. "The United States is a nation drunk with power," a Panamanian official told a group of South and Central American leaders shortly after the riots. "Panama's cause is the cause of all the Americas."[44] Many of his listeners agreed.

The second factor had to do with the canal's value. The Panama Canal had once been a military necessity, but times had changed. By the 1960s the US Navy was large enough to station plenty of ships in the Pacific—and plenty of ships, at the same time, in the Atlantic. Moving warships between the oceans was no longer essential. Moreover, the size of naval ships had grown steadily over the years, and the largest warships were now too large to fit through the canal. Commercially, the canal was losing its luster as well. More and more goods were being transported by train, truck, or airplane rather than by cargo ship. In short, the canal was becoming a convenience, not a requirement. Under these circumstances, ceding control of the canal to Panama did not look quite as foolish as it had years earlier.

A New Agreement

In the end the new realities of the canal, coupled with the international pressure on the United States to give Panama a better deal, pushed Johnson and his successors to agree to revise the existing treaty. Over the next decade or so, diplomats representing the United States and Panama met frequently to discuss what a new agreement would look like. At first the United States showed a willingness to share some of the responsibility of running the canal, but would go no further than that. As time passed, though, it became increasingly evident to most American government officials that the public relations cost of keeping the canal was too great. That concern, in turn, encouraged the United States to make further concessions to the Panamanian government.

In 1974 negotiators for the two sides finally reached a tentative agreement. The new treaty gave Panama a much larger share of the canal's tolls than before and provided that the two nations would jointly defend the canal if it should be attacked by another power. Of greater interest to the Panamanians, however, were two promises: a promise to dissolve the Canal Zone at some point in the future and another to turn the canal over to Panama after that. Exactly when those events would happen was still uncertain. But for the first time, the United States had agreed in principle to relinquish its rights to the canal and to the territory that surrounded it. All that remained was to hammer out those final details—and to pass the treaty on both sides.

WORDS IN CONTEXT
ratification
Approval by a legislative body.

Both goals, however, proved somewhat difficult to accomplish. In particular many Americans strongly disapproved of giving up control of the canal and eliminating the Canal Zone. Not only did they oppose the idea of giving away territory, they also worried that Panama might someday have a government that would be hostile to the United States—which would create problems for American ships trying to move through the waterway. In 1976 presidential candidate

Ronald Reagan made a strong appeal to scuttle the treaty. After all, as Reagan said frequently, the canal was not Panama's: "We bought it, we paid for it, it's ours."[45] Other leaders agreed, though not all as uncompromisingly as Reagan. "We should keep it," California politician

"ANOTHER DAY CLOSER"

The transfer of the Panama Canal to Panamanian control was set for December 31, 1999. As that date approached, a handful of American politicians argued that the US government should call off the transfer in the interest of national security. Some asserted that the Panamanian government could not be trusted to keep the canal functioning. And a few worried about connections between Panama and other countries hostile to the United States, most notably China.

Senator Robert Smith of New Hampshire was a particularly strong proponent of breaking the treaties signed by Carter and Torrijos. In October 1999 he gave an impassioned speech in Congress warning of the consequences of relinquishing the canal. "It's 84 more days" until the transfer, Smith said.

> We will come back next week . . . and it will be 79 days, or whatever it happens to be. But as each day ticks off, another day gone by—another day we haven't talked to [Panamanian] President Moscoso and we haven't tried to reopen the negotiations, and we are another day closer to turning the Panama Canal not over to the Panamanians, but to the Chinese Communists—and not a whimper from anybody in the State Department, or the President, the Defense Department, Presidential campaigns, or anywhere. So the days are getting short. I think that I have an obligation to tell the American people, on a day-to-day basis—remind them—about what is going on.

Few Americans paid attention, however, and the transfer went on as scheduled.

Congressional Record. Washington, DC: Government Printing Office, 1999, p. 24,534.

International leaders attend a 1978 ceremony where US president Jimmy Carter and General Omar Torrijos of Panama sign the Panama Canal treaty, promising to give the canal to the Panamanian government.

S.I. Hayakawa was fond of quipping, "we stole it fair and square."[46]

But Reagan lost his campaign bid in 1976 (though four years later he would win both the Republican nomination and the presidency), and Hayakawa eventually changed his mind about the treaty. Despite intense opposition from some Americans, negotiations continued. In September 1977 the two sides unveiled two new treaty proposals. One, the Neutrality Treaty, guaranteed that the canal would remain open to shipping from all nations. The other, called simply the Panama Canal Treaty, set a date for the handover of the canal to the Panamanians: December 31, 1999. American opponents of the treaties tried desperately to block ratification—by law both houses of Congress must approve a new treaty—but in the end they failed. In 1978, at a ceremony in Panama City, US president Jimmy Carter and General Omar Torrijos of Panama signed the documents.

That signing marked the beginning of the end of American control over the Panama Canal. In 1979 the Canal Zone was formally abolished, its territory being absorbed into Panama's. Over the next two decades, Panama gradually took on more and more responsibility over the waterway. Late in 1999, as planned, the two nations made the final transition. The last American soldiers stationed in Panama departed, and the canal was officially Panama's. "At last, Panama has reached sovereignty,"[47] rejoiced then-president Mireya Moscoso. The twentieth century was done—and with it the era of American control of the Panama Canal.

CHAPTER FIVE

The Future

In 2014 the Panama Canal reached its hundredth birthday. Though lessened somewhat in importance, it remains a remarkable and useful structure, a testament to the foresight of its planners and the skills of its builders. Today about fourteen thousand ships a year traverse the canal, carrying hundreds of millions of tons of cargo to ports across the world. Ships from countries as varied as China, Denmark, and Colombia are frequent sights along the waterway. Total revenues from canal tolls and other sources approach $2 billion a year. And the political conflicts that surrounded the canal during the twentieth century are no longer in play.

For a structure that was built a century ago, moreover, the Panama Canal is generally holding up well. Through the years workers have done a good job of maintaining the canal. Among other things, they have made sure that the gates of the locks continue to move efficiently, and they have kept silt and other materials from piling up at the bottom of the shipping lanes. The safety record along the canal has been outstanding. According to the Panama Canal Authority, which maintains and manages the canal, there are usually no more than ten or twelve accidents a year along the canal. This number represents a tiny percentage of the ships that pass through the locks. On the whole, both physically and financially, the Panama Canal is in fine shape.

Nonetheless, some significant issues surround the canal as it moves into its second century of use. The canal is threatened to at least some extent by continuing changes in the shipping industry. These changes are already limiting how the waterway is used, and they may well have an even greater effect on it in the future. Competition is another potential threat. Though there are currently no quick alternatives to the Panama Canal for ships needing to move between the Pacific and Atlantic Oceans, that may not remain true forever; it is entirely possible that a new canal may be built somewhere else in Central America at some point in the future. In the meantime, moreover, some shippers are choosing to avoid high canal tolls by sending ships on much longer journeys that do not involve a trip through Panama. How much this practice will impact canal revenues remains to be seen.

Traffic Jams

The process of moving ships through the Panama Canal has changed little since 1914. Today as in the past, tugboats push the larger ocean-going ships into position at the entrance to the canal; the use of tugs is a necessity because the ships are simply too large and unwieldy to move to the entrance without assistance, especially when winds are high and currents are strong. To go through the locks, the ships are attached to engines known as mules, which are used to guide the ships in the right direction and keep them from bumping against the sides of the lock. Once in the lock, vessels are lifted and lowered as water flows into—or out of—the chambers behind the gates. When the gates are opened, the ship makes its way forward to the next lock and repeats the process. Upon reaching sea level again, it can head once more for the open ocean.

WORDS IN CONTEXT
moored
Anchored.

In good weather and without excessive traffic, the total trip through the canal usually takes between eight and ten hours—about the same length of time it took the *Ancon* to make the first official transit of the canal a century ago. However, not all ships can move at that speed. The roughly fourteen thousand ships that make the transit each year represent an average of close to forty ships a day.

A large container ship passes through the Panama Canal. The largest ships that can fit through the canal usually must travel single file.

The canal's capacity—the largest number of ships it can realistically handle in the course of a day—is about thirty-five. Most days, then, the number of ships transiting the canal is slightly greater than the ideal maximum. Unfortunately, even a small uptick in the number of ships trying to traverse the canal can cause stress on the system and lead to lengthy backups. "During much of the year," writes a reporter, "dozens of ships are moored off each coast, waiting a day or longer to enter the canal."[48]

Most of the traffic backup is a function of the large number of ships, but the size of ships plays a role, too. Many of the ships that travel through the canal today are of a type known as Panamax. The word, which combines *Panama* and *maximum*, refers to the largest ships that can fit in the locks of the Panama Canal: approximately 965 feet (294 m) in length, 106 feet (32.3 m) in width, and 39.5 feet (12 m) from bottom to waterline. But though Panamax ships can fit through the canal, they often cannot pass one another in opposite directions;

parts of the canal are not wide enough to fit two Panamax ships side by side. To manage traffic properly, then, it is often necessary to hold a Panamax ship near one approach to the canal while another similarly sized ship crosses the isthmus in the opposite direction.

The delays are a significant issue. They cost shippers both money and time. They are wasteful, too; plenty of valuable fuel is lost while ships are lined up in the approach channels. Perhaps most significant, the delays are costly to the canal authority as well. Officials believe that more ships would be willing to pay the toll to pass through the waterway if not for the seemingly interminable waits. In the past, canal officials have tried several ways to address the delays. Most notably, perhaps, they have often allowed shippers to pay extra—up to several hundred thousand dollars—to move to the front of the line and go through right away. While that solution has increased revenue, it does little to solve the underlying problem.

Panamax and Beyond

At the same time that they worry about excess traffic, though, canal officials also must contend with the seemingly opposite problem: a projected drop in the number of ships heading into the canal. The reason for this change involves technology. The canal was built to accommodate the largest ships being constructed at the start of the twentieth century. It was true that some of these ships could barely squeeze into the locks; but in 1914 no one had built a ship that was too big to make its way into the locks. And as far as anyone knew, no one ever would. The technology, fuels, and materials of the time meant that such a ship would be too heavy and too unwieldy to maneuver easily.

> **WORDS IN CONTEXT**
> Panamax
> *The largest type of ship that fits through the locks of the Panama Canal.*

By the 1930s technology had begun to improve. Still, few people were interested in building ships that exceeded the size of the Panama Canal's locks. The limits set by the locks, one website says, encouraged companies to design vessels "strictly in accordance with the dimensions (width, length, and depth) of the lock chambers."[49] Even when some Japanese shipbuilders began to build warships that were slightly bigger than the lock capacity at Panama, the rest of the world did not immediately follow their lead. Panamax, it seemed, would remain a firm limit on the size of ships.

But in fact, it did not. As time went on, the opportunities extended by new materials and new technologies could not be denied. It soon became easy to build relatively stable and speedy vessels that far exceeded the size of earlier ships. The average cargo ship today, for instance, is considerably larger than the freighters and warships of a century ago. So are some passenger ships. The Maersk shipping company alone operates nearly one hundred ships that qualify as "post-Panamax"—that is, they are larger than Panamax vessels and therefore too large to fit through the canal. By one estimate, more than a third of the commercial ships being built in the 2010s cannot transit the canal for just this reason. As one website explains, "Panamax ships . . . are no longer the industry standard."[50]

The value of these enormous ships lies in their efficiency. The ships' great size makes them able to carry more cargo at correspondingly lower cost than smaller ships can manage. For their owners, the fact that post-Panamax ships cannot navigate through the Panama Canal seems like a small price to pay for the increased efficiency—and the resulting monetary savings. Many of these ships are used on routes that keep them entirely within one ocean. Others are sent around Cape Horn, journey past the southern tip of Africa, or move through the larger Suez Canal in the Middle East. Clearly, the Panama Canal Authority suffers financial harm if a large number of oceangoing ships cannot possibly go through the canal. And if the trend toward larger ships continues, the problem will only grow worse.

Expansion

In 2007, hoping to address the twin problems of big ships and long delays, canal officials launched a major renovation project. This proj-

EXPANSION ISSUES

The Panama Canal expansion has generally gone smoothly, but like most large projects, it has been bedeviled by some problems. On several occasions, for instance, labor unrest has temporarily stopped work on the upgrades. In the spring of 2014, for example, many construction workers walked off the job in hopes of winning a pay hike of 35 percent, a figure they justified in part by pointing to Panama's high inflation rate. Panamanian leaders were not pleased. "Each day of the strike brings new delays that harm the reputation and trust in the country as [a] reliable center for transport," warned the Panama Canal Authority. After two weeks, however, the two sides negotiated a smaller wage increase, and work began again.

Funding has sometimes been a problem as well. In the winter of 2014 it was discovered that the construction was about $1.6 billion over budget. The canal authority and several European construction companies argued for two months about who was responsible for these cost overruns, and during this time work came to a halt. Finally, the two sides agreed to submit to binding arbitration, with each accepting some financial responsibility for the situation, and work resumed in early March.

Quoted in Eric Sabo, "Panama Election Contest Tightens as Strike Halts Canal Expansion," *Bloomberg Businessweek*, May 2, 2014. www.businessweek.com.

---

ect, known as the Panama Canal Expansion, is intended to double the existing capacity of the waterway and make it accessible to many of the world's largest ships. The major change will be to add a third lane with newly designed locks about 25 percent longer and 50 percent wider than the originals. The largest ships that fit in locks of this size will be called "New Panamax" vessels. While some of the biggest supertankers and cargo ships will still be too large to transit the canal, well over half of the post-Panamax ships in the world will be able to make the journey along the waterway once construction is done.

To properly accommodate these larger ships, the expansion project requires other work as well. Since post-Panamax ships typically

The Panama Canal Expansion project, photographed in 2012, was to add a third lane to the original canal. The estimated cost of expansion was $5.25 billion.

are heavier than smaller ones, they ride lower in the water and need to move through deeper channels. Thus, the entrances to both ends of the canal are being dredged, as are some of the shallower portions of the canal itself. The canal is being widened, too, to allow ships to pass one another without incident—an improvement that canal officials expect to speed up traffic significantly. And because operating the larger locks will require more water, the level of Gatun Lake is being raised by about 1.5 feet (0.5 m).

The notion of a canal expansion is not new. In fact, the idea dates back to the 1930s. Recognizing at the time that the size of battleships could ultimately increase, several American engineers suggested that another set of locks would be a good idea. For various reasons, including a lack of funds, no one acted on the plan at first. But in 1939 construction on a third set actually got under way. The outbreak of World War II later that year limited both the time and money available for the project, however, and work was stopped in 1942 without much having been accomplished. Following the war, the United States decided not to resume the project. The subject came up again later in the twentieth century, as transition to Panamanian control was beginning, and was tabled once more. Not until 2007 did work on a third set of locks move past the beginning stages.

Progress

The expansion is a major undertaking. The estimated cost of the project is $5.25 billion, which is being borrowed from banks; the money is expected to be repaid out of tolls from the newly opened locks. As with construction of the original canal, the expansion requires the excavation of many tons of earth and the building of tall concrete locks. Of course, workers of today use machinery that is much more effective than the relatively primitive steam shovels, railroad cars, and dynamite charges of a century ago. "Giant hydraulic excavators scoop blasted rock into a parade of earth movers that dump it topside on a slowly growing mountain of rubble,"[51] one eyewitness writes, describing the earth-moving techniques of the 2010s.

Despite the complexity of the expansion and several nagging issues involving funding and labor, officials expect to finish by mid-2015. "Most of the work [on] the various projects has already been completed,"[52] the Panama Canal Authority posted on its website in the spring of 2014. Certainly canal officials are eagerly awaiting the opening of the new third lane. They project that the expansion will increase the canal's capacity from about thirty-five ships a day to approximately fifty; this will in turn add revenue, sharply reduce delays, and make the canal a more palatable option for maritime shippers all across the world. If they are right, ports elsewhere around the globe will benefit as well from the increased volume of traffic making its way through the canal. The port of Charleston, South Carolina, for instance, is spending more

> **WORDS IN CONTEXT**
> maritime
> *Having to do with the sea.*

than $1 billion to upgrade its facilities in the expectation that a larger Panama Canal will mean a rise in shipping in general.

The project has been controversial, however. Some people have questioned the Panamanian government's insistence that the canal will be far more profitable with the third set of locks. They worry that the government has overestimated the number of ships that will come to Panama to transit a larger canal. Other critics of the plan are worried that the project will have a sharply negative effect on the environment. Water is a particular issue. Many fear that the expansion will contaminate groundwater and reduce water quality, and the project's opponents often mention their concern that the water of Gatun Lake—which is used for drinking by residents of the area around the canal—will become excessively salty, potentially compromising the health of Panama's people.

Competition

The biggest threat facing the Panama Canal today, however, might not be the long lines, the high tolls, or the increasing number of ships too large to pass through the antiquated locks. Instead, the central problem for the canal authority may be the wealth of alternatives to the Panama Canal in today's world. Land and air transportation have become cheaper, more reliable, and more widely available in the years since the canal was first opened. More and more goods are sent by truck and by airplane. And merchants who continue to send goods by ship have been increasingly likely to use other existing routes, such as the Suez Canal. Both trends are unfavorable to the continued growth of the canal.

Perhaps more alarming for members of the Panama Canal Authority, however, is the possibility that thousands of ships might forsake the canal altogether for a new and different route. Climate change in the Arctic is gradually opening up the Northwest Passage, for instance—the northern waterway eagerly sought by explorers

Climate change is drastically changing the Northwest Passage (pictured here) leaving it free of ice for the first time in more than three centuries. Such changes may allow ships to access another shipping route.

for three centuries. Impenetrable to ships since the 1600s, the passage, which leads across the top of Canada and Alaska, is much less choked with ice than it used to be. In the fall of 2008, a commercial ship was able to make its way through most of the passage. "There was no ice whatsoever,"[53] one crew member said afterward. As climate change continues, it is possible that the passage will become ever more appealing to shippers, cutting further into the Panama Canal's business.

And there is no guarantee that Panama will always have the only canal in the Americas. For many years various groups have proposed building a new canal somewhere else in the region. A second canal across Central America or northern Colombia would face many issues, beginning with time and money. It would take years to plan and build such a canal, and constructing one would cost countless billions of dollars. In a time of austere budgets and a need to give shareholders

CONCERNS ABOUT A COMPETING CANAL

In recent years Nicaragua has enthusiastically pursued investors who might build a canal across its territory. Constructing a canal through Nicaragua would benefit the country in several ways, notably by putting people to work and by charging tolls on ships making the passage. However, the possibility of a canal has sparked a number of concerns as well, perhaps the most pressing of them centered on the environment.

One particular concern involves Lake Nicaragua, an existing body of water in the Nicaraguan interior that could easily be incorporated into the canal. Too shallow for oceangoing vessels, the lake would need extensive dredging to make it deep enough for canal traffic. So much dredging, however, could have negative effects on the water in the lake. "The initial digging," explains an expert, "would create a huge sediment issue that would be bad for water quality in the lake and the wetlands around it."

Wildlife is another concern. It is not clear how the dredging of Lake Nicaragua would affect fish and other animals native to the lake. The nearby forests, meanwhile, are home to a variety of mammals, some of them already under stress from human encroachment on what had once been wilderness. Constructing a canal would certainly be harmful to these populations, though no one knows how serious the effect would be. It remains to be seen whether these environmental considerations will make it more difficult to build a waterway that will compete with the Panama Canal.

Quoted in Greg Miller, "Why the Plan to Dig a Canal Across Nicaragua Could Be a Very Bad Idea," *Wired*, February 26, 2014. www.wired.com.

quick results, it may well be that no such canal will ever be built. And so far, nothing has come of any of these plans.

But that could change, because a second canal could prove extremely lucrative to those who build it and pay for it. The country providing land for the canal would certainly benefit: Canal construction would offer the nation's people plenty of jobs, and the country could collect tolls once the canal was in place. Banks and other investors who chose to provide funding for this project would benefit, too, by sharing in any profits the canal might make. As long as national governments and potential investors see a possible market for a second canal, discussion will follow.

A Nicaraguan Canal?

Indeed, in 2013 a company based in Hong Kong negotiated an agreement with Nicaragua's government to build a canal across Nicaraguan territory. The canal is expected to cost $40 billion and take five years to build, with construction planned to begin late in 2014. Like past proposals for new canals in the Central American region, this project may never be finished. Certainly, the process of building a waterway across Nicaragua will be complicated. If it is completed, however, that would be bad news for the Panama Canal. Since Nicaragua lies north of Panama, a Nicaraguan canal would be a more direct route for ships traveling almost anywhere in the Northern Hemisphere. A Nicaraguan canal, built with today's supertankers and gigantic cargo ships in mind, would be easier to traverse than the canal in Panama—even the expanded version set to open in 2015. And competition from Nicaragua would almost surely drive down the tolls the Panama Canal could charge.

These concerns are in the future, however. For now, canal officials are content to expand the waterway's capacity by adding the third set of locks, dredging where necessary, and widening the channel where possible. No matter what happens in Canada or Nicaragua, these improvements to the Panama Canal are very likely to pay off in the next few years, both by attracting ships that cannot currently transit the canal and by making the experience of passing through the waterway easier for those that can. In the short run, at least, the Panama Canal will no doubt maintain its popularity as the quickest route between the oceans. And it may well keep its status as one of the most remarkable—and useful—structures on earth for many years to come.

SOURCE NOTES

Chapter One: A Plan

1. Quoted in Anthony Brandt, *The Man Who Ate His Boots*. New York: Knopf, 2010, p. 61.
2. Quoted in *Panama Canal Review*. May 4, 1954.
3. Quoted in Julie Greene, *The Canal Builders*. New York: Penguin, 2009, p. 21.
4. Quoted in Robert C. Harding, *The History of Panama*. New York: Greenwood, 2006, p. 29.
5. Quoted in Jeremy Sherman Snapp, *Destiny by Design: The Construction of the Panama Canal*. Lopez Island, WA: Pacific Heritage, 2000, p. 11.
6. Snapp, *Destiny by Design*, p. 11.
7. Quoted in Greene, *The Canal Builders*, p. 22.
8. Quoted in Greene, *The Canal Builders*, p. 25.
9. Quoted in Snapp, *Destiny by Design*, p. 11.
10. Board of Consulting Engineers for the Panama Canal, *Report of the Board of Consulting Engineers for the Panama Canal*. Washington, DC: Government Printing Office, 1906, p. 22.
11. Quoted in Edmund Morris, *The Rise of Theodore Roosevelt*. New York: Modern Library, 1979, p. 116.

Chapter Two: Construction

12. Theodore Roosevelt, *Theodore Roosevelt: An Autobiography*. New York: Scribner, 1920, p. 543.
13. *Canal Record*, Ancon (Panama), Canal Zone, "Longevity Regulations," September 4, 1907, p. 6.
14. *Canal Record*, "Immigrants from Barbados," July 28, 1909, p. 378.
15. *Canal Record*, "Material in Slides," July 28, 1909, p. 377.
16. Snapp, *Destiny by Design*, p. 98.
17. *Canal Record*, "Movement and Repair of Trains," September 4, 1907, p. 2.

18. Snapp, *Destiny by Design*, p. 120.
19. *Canal Record*, "Watertight Lock Gates," August 6, 1913, p. 425.
20. *Canal Record*, "Completion of Lock Gates," January 28, 1914, p. 216.
21. *Canal Record*, "Steamship 'Cristobal' Makes Test Trip Between Entrance Channels," August 5, 1914, p. 493.
22. Quoted in *Canal Record*, "Canal Opened to Traffic," August 19, 1914, p. 521.

Chapter Three: The Workers

23. Quoted in David McCullough, *The Path Between the Seas: The Creation of the Panama Canal, 1870–1914*. New York: Simon and Schuster, 1977, p. 580.
24. Quoted in Charles L.G. Anderson, *Old Panama and Castilla del Oro*. Boston: Page, 1914, p. 471.
25. PBS, *American Experience*, "Yellow Fever and Malaria in the Canal." www.pbs.org.
26. *Canal Record*, "Yellow Fever Case from Guayaquil," March 11, 1908, p. 224.
27. Quoted in McCullough, *The Path Between the Seas*, p. 580.
28. *Canal Record*, "Fatal Dynamite Explosion," July 28, 1909, p. 378.
29. Quoted in McCullough, *The Path Between the Seas*, pp. 580–81.
30. Quoted in Greene, *The Canal Builders*, pp. 78–79.
31. Frederic Jennings Haskin, *The Panama Canal*. Garden City, NY: Doubleday, Page, 1913, p. 159.
32. Greene, *The Canal Builders*, p. 63.
33. Quoted in Greene, *The Canal Builders*, p. 98.
34. Quoted in Greene, *The Canal Builders*, p. 70.
35. *Canal Record*, "Independent Order of Panamanian Kangaroos," April 29, 1908, p. 275.
36. Quoted in *Canal Record*, "Tea Rooms for the Zone?," January 22, 1908, p. 163.
37. *Canal Record*, "Sports and Games: Baseball," September 4, 1907, p. 5.

Chapter Four: Transition

38. *Canal Record*, "Summary of First Nine Years of Canal Operation," August 15, 1923, p. 1.

39. Quoted in Greene, *The Canal Builders*, pp. 323–24.

40. Quoted in Greene, *The Canal Builders*, p. 330.

41. Quoted in Greene, *The Canal Builders*, p. 328.

42. Quoted in *Canal Record*, "Re-Employment of Silver Employees," March 3, 1920, p. 425.

43. Quoted in Ashley Byrne, "Fifty Years Ago This Week," PRI, January 10, 2014. www.pri.org.

44. Quoted in Susan Dudley Gold, *The Panama Canal Transfer*. Austin, TX: Raintree Steck-Vaughn, 1999, p. 61.

45. Quoted in Kenneth E. Morris, *Unfinished Revolution: Daniel Ortega and Nicaragua's Struggle for Liberation*. Chicago: Chicago Review, 2010, p. 139.

46. Quoted in Leroy Aarons, "Samuel Ichiye Hayakawa Is a 72-Year-Old Freshman Senator of Many Hats—and Parts," *People*, October 2, 1978. www.people.com.

47. Quoted in Randy Krehbiel, "Unlocking Control." *Cobblestone*, April 2001, p. 41.

Chapter Five: The Future

48. Henry Fountain, "Panama Adding a Wider Shortcut for Shipping," *New York Times*, August 16, 2011. www.nytimes.com.

49. Maritime Connector, "Panamax and New Panamax." http://maritime-connector.com.

50. PBS, "American Experience: Then & Now: The Panama Canal." www.pbs.org.

51. Fountain, "Panama Adding a Wider Shortcut for Shipping."

52. Panama Canal Expansion, "Frequently Asked Questions," 2014. http://micanaldepanama.com.

53. *CBC News*, "First Commercial Ship Sails Through Northwest Passage," November 28, 2008. http://www.cbc.ca.

FACTS ABOUT THE PANAMA CANAL

Geography

- The Panama Canal is about 48 miles (77 km) in length.
- The highest elevation along the Panama Canal is 85 feet (26 m) above sea level.
- The canal is roughly on a north–south axis, with the Pacific entrance being slightly to the east of the Atlantic entrance.
- About 15 miles (24 km) of the canal are formed by Gatun Lake, an artificial lake created when the canal was constructed.
- The Culebra Cut, the most difficult part of the canal route to be excavated, is about 8 miles (13 km) in length.

Use and Tolls

- Approximately eight hundred thousand ships passed through the canal between 1914 and 2007.
- Currently, about fourteen thousand ships pass through the canal each year.
- Under ideal conditions, it takes eight to ten hours for a ship to pass through the Panama Canal.
- The minimum toll charged for a ship of up to 50 feet (15 m) in length is $1,300.
- As of 2014 the highest toll paid to traverse the canal was $375,600, by a cruise ship in 2010.
- The lowest toll ever paid to transit the Panama Canal was thirty-six cents, paid by adventurer Richard Halliburton, who swam the length of the canal in 1928.

Locks

- The canal includes six sets of locks, three on the Pacific side and three on the Atlantic side.
- The locks are about 110 feet (34 m) wide and 1,050 feet (320 m) long.
- The lock gates are an average of 6.5 feet (2 m) thick and 66 feet (20 m) high.

History

- The canal originally cost the United States $375 million.
- The French excavated about 30 million cubic yards (23 million cu. m) of earth before abandoning the canal in 1888.
- The United States excavated at least 170 million cubic yards (130 million cu. m) of earth while building the canal.

FOR FURTHER RESEARCH

Books

Sylvia Engdahl, ed., *Building the Panama Canal*. Detroit: Greenhaven, 2012.

Julie Greene, *The Canal Builders*. New York: Penguin, 2009.

Noel Maurer and Carlos Yu, *The Big Ditch*. Princeton, NJ: Princeton, 2011.

Matthew Parker, *Panama Fever*. New York: Anchor, 2009.

Janet Pascal, *What Is the Panama Canal?* New York: Grosset and Dunlap, 2014.

Sue Vander Hook, *Building the Panama Canal*. Edina, MN: ABDO, 2010.

Websites

American Experience: Panama Canal, PBS (www.pbs.org/wgbh/americanexperience/films/panama). Information about the project, the workers, and the political maneuvering behind the building of the canal.

Canal Museum.com (www.canalmuseum.com). Links to photographs, documents, and other materials focused on the building and running of the canal.

Canal Record, University of Florida Digital Collections (http://ufdc.ufl.edu/UF00097368/allvolumes2). The complete run of the *Canal Record*, the newspaper of the Canal Zone beginning in 1907 and continuing through construction and beyond.

Make the Dirt Fly! **Smithsonian Institution Libraries** (www.sil.si
.edu/Exhibitions/Make-the-Dirt-Fly). An exhibition of photographs and information about the canal.

Panama Canal (www.pancanal.com/eng). The official website of the
organization that operates and maintains the Panama Canal; includes
a simulation of how the canal works.

Panama Canal Expansion (http://micanaldepanama.com/expansion).
Information about the Panama Canal expansion project that began
in 2007.

INDEX

Note: Boldface page numbers indicate illustrations.

ABOUT THE AUTHOR

Stephen Currie has published dozens of books and other educational materials. His works for ReferencePoint Press include *The Medieval Castle*, *Goblins*, and *The Future of Hydropower*. He has taught at levels ranging from kindergarten to college. He lives in New York State.

FRIENDS FREE LIBRARY
GERMANTOWN FRIENDS LIBRARY
5418 Germantown Avenue
Philadelphia, PA 19144
215-951-2355

Each borrower is responsible for all items
checked out on his/her library card, for
fines on materials kept overtime, and
replacing any lost or damaged materials.